THE SECRET OF HIGH IMPACT LEADERS

5 PROVEN LEADERSHIP ACTIONS TO MAKE YOUR TEAM HIGHLY ENGAGED AND PRODUCTIVE

THE SECRET OF HIGH IMPACT LEADERS

5 PROVEN LEADERSHIP ACTIONS TO MAKE YOUR TEAM HIGHLY ENGAGED AND PRODUCTIVE

YOSHIHARU MATSUI

Copyright © 2018 Yoshiharu Matsui

Publishing Services by Happy Self Publishing
www.happyselfpublishing.com

Year: 2018

All rights reserved. No reproduction, transmission or copy of this publication can be made without the written consent of the author in accordance with the provision of the Copyright Acts. Any person doing so will be liable to civil claims and criminal prosecution.

TABLE OF CONTENT

Introduction 1

Chapter 1: Keys to Happy and Productive Team 5

Chapter 2: Key Success Factors of High-Performance Teams 33

Chapter 3: Leadership Matters 63

Chapter 4: Leadership Action 1 – Envision...... 87

Chapter 5: Leadership Action 2 - Engage...... 117

Chapter 6: Leadership Action 3 - Empower... 153

Chapter 7: Leadership Action 4 - Enable Members... 183

Chapter 8: Leaders Action 5 – Enhance Systems and Environment 233

Chapter 9: Putting It All Together 285

Chapter 10: Upgrading Your Skills as a Leader 333

Bibliography 353

Author Bio 359

Introduction

As poor employee engagement is causing inefficiency, poor productivity, higher cost, and lower profit, many organizations have been trying various ways to improve employee engagement and organization performance for decades. However, Gallup surveys have continuously indicated poor employee engagement results since 2000. So, employee engagement continues to be a key theme for many organizations and team leaders.

I started my corporate life as an assistant marketing manager for Vicks, a pharmaceutical company, and managed several cough and cold products for a number of years. I was a very happy and motivated person, and I initiated several new projects to lead the brand to success, focusing on revenue and market share. I thought I was also a good manager building both business and my team.

As Vicks was acquired by Procter and Gamble (P&G), I moved to the P&G marketing (Advertising) organization. A few years after moving, I got to know my reality. My boss called me one day and told me what my people were thinking about me as a manager, so-called member feedback or 360 feedback. While I thought I was a good boss, my members' feedback was not all good. While I had several strong points, my people wanted me to be more appreciative and supportive, and also be less critical and perfectionist – a bit shocking and an eye-opening moment for me as a leader.

I moved to the Human Resources (HR) division and started my leadership and organization development work more than 20 years ago; my boss had moved to HR, and he pulled me there from marketing. As the company has been one of leaders in development and delivery, I learned a lot about how to effectively lead and manage members.

Since I moved to HR, I have supported many teams, functions, business units, and organizations to improve their employee and organization performance for the last two decades, as both an internal and external leadership development and organization change facilitator. During a course for leadership development and organization change support, I learned, tested, and identified many key success factors, as well as unsuccessful factors, for team and organization effectiveness. Most of my programs have been very effective and successful in delivering target change, such as 30 - 50% growth of employee engagement in just one year, regardless of types of organizations.

Target readers of this book are any leaders and managers who want to improve or further strengthen their team performance, regardless of their level of experience - from experienced to a newly promoted, to even those who want to become a manager.

After reading this book, you will be able to (a) understand key success factors for building a highly engaged and productive team, (b) learn key five leadership actions and principles to building a high-performance team, and (c) identify specific action plans to enhance team engagement and productivity as well as your team leadership effectiveness.

This book is composed of 10 chapters. Chapter 1 discusses current challenges in teams and organizations. Chapter 2 reveals the key characteristics of high-performance teams. Chapter 3 identifies the foundations of team leadership – what it takes to be a high-performance leader. From Chapter 4 through to 8, I introduce leaders' five key actions to make teams happier and more productive – engaging (Chapter 4), envisioning (Chapter 5), empowering (Chapter 6), enabling (Chapter 7), and enhancing systems and environments (Chapter 8). Chapter 9 suggests typical team development steps toward building a high-performance team. Finally, Chapter 10 discusses how to upgrade team leadership competency to successfully implement the five key leaders' actions.

I am sure you will have several important takeaways and be able to identify specific action plans through reading this book. I look forward to hearing from you about your successes in building an engaged and productive team in 3 - 6 months.

Chapter 1

Keys to Happy and Productive Team

High-performance teams have many competent members who deliver good results. Reflecting your work experience to date, who are some of those high performers? What are their key characteristics and factors for high performance?

When I ask those questions, most managers respond with a wide variety of technical competencies, problem-solving, and interpersonal skills. I am sure your response to the above questions would be similar, perhaps, with a different set of skills. Competence levels can certainly influence a person's performance. For example, salespeople who have mastered selling skills and have a great understanding of their market along with good product knowledge can most likely sell very well compared to those with limited sales and market experiences.

Is competency (skills, knowledge) enough to achieve great results? Many learning and development professionals and consultants say that it's not only the competence level, but also the attitudes or mindset that drives performance. Dr. Ken Blanchard, a leadership and performance development guru, articulates that members' performance depends on both competency and commitment, or the skill and motivation levels. So, the salespeople with great selling skills and market and product knowledge may not sell well if they are not motivated to sell. Or athletes with great athletic skills and sports knowledge may not perform their best when they are not committed or not confident to perform.

So, we need to build both the competence and commitment to become high performing. This is particularly true in situations or settings where individuals work independently. However, in a team setting where members work interdependently and collaboratively with other team members, what other factors come in to play and influence each member's performance?

It's the context or environment in which members work that influences each team member and the team's performance. Some of key variables of context are:

- the member composition
- the relationship and collaboration level
- information sharing
- decision-making methods among them
- the robustness of work processes
- the user-friendliness of systems and policies
- the team structure

Other variables include the conditions of the workplace, such as the room temperature, lighting, humidity, the office size, and the height of partitions.

$$Performance = Competence \times Commitment \times Context$$

So, if we want to strengthen our team performance, we need to build competence (ability and knowledge), commitment (engagement, willingness, and confidence), and context (team, process, system, environment, and culture).

So, if the performance is an issue for your team, which one of the three factors might be affecting the performance most? Then, what specific actions do you want to take to increase the team performance?

I will cover those in the next section.

The Power of Engagement

Employee engagement has been a buzzword for about a couple of decades among leaders as well as Human Resource Development professionals. A Gallup poll in 2015 showed that only 15% of workforce worldwide is actively engaged (http://news.gallup.com/opinion/gallup/216155/reasons-why-employee-engagement-programs-fall-short.aspx?g_source=EMPLOYEE_ ENGAGEMENT&g_medium=topic&g_campaign =tiles).

Merriam-Webster defines engagement as "emotional involvement or commitment" (https://www. merriam-webster.com/dictionary/engagement The). So, when members are highly engaged in their work, they feel connected to it and more motivated about working on their projects, and also taking ownership to accomplish their task. According to the OECD report, majority of workers spend 36 hours or more on their work per week without including work-related matters, such as commuting, isn't it pity that the majority of the workforce is not engaged in what they do for work? (See https://stats.oecd.org/Index.aspx?DataSetCode=ANHRS%20)

A Gallup survey also indicates that employee engagement has a direct influence on an organization's productivity – the level of performance, efficiency, yield, defects, absenteeism, and so on (https://news.gallup.com/businessjournal/163130/employee-engagement-drives-growth.aspx). So, the lower the employee engagement, the lower the productivity of the organization or team. In addition to reducing productivity, poor employee engagement leads to increased turnover cost, which results in additional hiring costs estimated at about 1.5times an employee's annual salary (https://www.inc.com/suzanne-lucas/why-employee-turnover-is-so-costly.html).
While we have seen a marginal improvement in the last several years in the U.S. (29% of those actively engaged in 2010 has increased to 33% in 2016), most of the U.S. workforce is still dis-

engaged (https://www.theemployeeapp.com/gallup-2017-employee-engagement-report-results-nothing-changed/). Gallup estimated that, in the U.S., the annual cost of actively disengaged employees can be around $450 to $600 billion per year, indicating that managers and leaders have a lot to do to turn around this trend.

The above Gallup engagement survey categorizes workforce into three groups – the actively engaged, the disengaged, and the actively disengaged. If you divide your members into these 3 categories, which members are in actively engaged, who are fully motivated and committed to achieving their tasks? Which members are working without showing much motivation or commitment? Who, if any, are actively disengaged, working against your team mission and values? What signs have you seen for you to be able to categorize your members into those three groups?

Imagine that all your members become highly engaged - more committed, motivated, and productive. What kind of new attitudes and behaviors would you see from them? And, what changes would you be able to see in your team's performance and productivity? You will certainly be able to see significant increases in your team's performance as a result of having all members highly engaged in the work.

So, what is influencing the level of employee engagement and commitment anyway? Now we will be looking into human needs and motivation factors that can affect people's engagement level.

What Motivates Members to Keep Working for the Company?

There are lots of challenges and difficulties in working in the current volatile, uncertain, complex, and ambiguous (VUCA) workplace - especially, when people are asked for more, faster, and better (while with fewer resources) to cope with a wide variety of organizational changes and challenges, such as cost-saving, lean manufacturing, delayering, restructuring, mergers and acquisitions, and management change. Many of those changes could create anxiety, stress, and frustration, which could negatively impact employee engagement.

Despite those challenging situations, why do some members stay with the company? The answer may be different depending on the industry or function. When I ask this question to a group of managers in financial business, many managers respond, "It's the pay." When asking those in the service industry, managers say, "It's the work conditions and/or workload." Or managers in the fast-growing information technology industries may say, "It's the perks and benefits, including free food, drinks, and relaxation facilities." So, how do you think your members would respond to the question of why they keep working for the team or the company?

Research done globally by Career System International (http://whatkeepsyou.csiprogram.com/Finished.aspx; April 30, 2018) indicates the top 10 reasons for employees to stay and thrive in their company are as follows; (% of those who responded).

The Reasons for Keeping Working for the Company

1. Exciting, meaningful or challenging work
   37.6%

2. Supportive management, good boss
   11.7%

3. Being recognized, valued, and respected
   10.0%

4. Career growth, learning and development
   9.9%

5. Job location 5.8%

6. Fair pay 5.3%

7. Job security and stability 5.2%

8. A flexible work environment 4.7%

9. Pride in the organization, its mission and product 3.4%

10. Fun, enjoyable work environment 2.2%

What do the above findings tell us? Contrary to some managers' speculations, pay does not appear in the top 5 reasons. Perks do not show up even among the top 10. The number one response is meaningful and exciting work. So, the top motivating factor is the job they are doing day in and day out, and it's an intrinsic factor. The number 2 response is about their boss – a supportive, caring, and respectful boss. This clearly indicates the importance of boss to motivate the team to thrive. The third reason is about recognition and respect from others in the workplace. As Maslow indicated, recognition is a basic human need that many of us look for especially when the job done well. The fourth reason is a career development and personal or professional growth - how they perceive their growth, learning and development and how they can identify their future with the current organization as they grow. The reasons that follow are mostly related to work conditions or external factors that are unrelated to a job itself, such as job location, fun work environments, and pay.

Motivational Needs in the Workplace

The above research indicates the key motivational factors are more intrinsic and closely related to the work itself. Let's review some of the key factors that help keep members motivated with their work.

1. **Challenging and meaningful work** - it is the number one reason for people to stay in the job or with the company. People want to work on a task that is meaningful to them, or something that challenges their thinking and capacity to contribute to others. Conversely, if members don't feel their job is meaningful, they will likely experience emotional distress, defensiveness, lower mood, and lack of engagement. The lack of challenging work will simply make people bored, prevent them from growing, and eventually result in high employee turnover. Research on person-job fit also indicates a good job fit and doing what one is good at can lead to enhanced motivation and better performance, a higher job satisfaction, greater self-esteem, all of which result in higher employee retention (https://www.researchgate.net/publication/309464801_An_Empirical_Analysis_of_The_Relationship_Between_Person-Job_Fit_and_Employee_Performance?enrichId=rgreq-e6dba798eb764638418b31358a1eb6c4-XXX&enrichSource=Y292ZXJQYWdlOzMwO

TQ2NDgwMTtBUzo0MjE3NTcxMTE4MDM5
MDhAMTQ3NzU2NjEzOTc5Nw%3D%3D&el
=1_x_3&_esc=publicationCoverPdf).

2. **Supportive boss** - This includes the manager's encouragement, care, and actual support for members to do a good job and develop themselves. A good boss communicates and engages with members to understand their needs and concerns before problems happen. A better boss assigns a member a meaningful and challenging task that helps them grow. Manager's developmental support could be providing feedback or coaching and training, which will satisfy members' growth needs.

3. **Recognition** – Recognition helps enhance our self-esteem. We feel good and a bit excited when our work is recognized. Managers' recognition motivates employees to further excel in their performance and overachieve their target results. Suppose no one recognizes what you do no matter how hard you've tried you may not feel any self-worth working on the task. For me, that would be a very stressful and discouraging workplace, and I may likely quit the job.

4. **Self-development and mastery with career growth** – The above survey findings also indicate people want to see and feel themselves grow in their competencies. Employees want to increase their self-worth, technical expertise, and professionalism. The more they get closer to mastery, the more effort they put in to become even better and achieve better results, which can also help develop their career. Research on the impact of employee development indicates fair access to development and growth opportunities will increase employees' goal commitment (Bartlet and Kang, 2004). This is an upward spiral and makes people feel good about themselves, meeting their intrinsic, motivational needs. I have seen many people who have received lots of professional development opportunities in their companies, and many of them said they even felt the need to give back to the company and passed several headhunters' seducing calls.

So, key motivational factors are meaningful work, recognition, developmental support, and a sense of growth. How many those motivational factors do your members experience at work?

Summary of the Top 4 Motivational Factors

1. Exciting, meaningful or challenging work

2. Supportive management, good boss

3. Being recognized, valued and respected

4. Career growth, learning and development

Fundamental Human Needs

In addition to motivational needs, there are more fundamental human needs to be satisfied to build an engaging and productive team. Recent studies identified good relationships along with psychological and physiological safety are fundamental needs (Ariani, 2015; https://www.tandfonline.com/doi/full/10.1080/15427609.2016.1141283).

Relationships - This factor can influence members' performance as well as the level of engagement. As the base for good relationships, respect and care are important factors to maintain a healthy team.

1. **Relationships** – A good relationship with the boss and colleagues is an essential factor for happily and stress-free work. Good relationships in the team help members communicate openly, share necessary information in a timely manner, and move the project forward smoothly. Conversely, a poor or a lack of social relationships can cause critical problems to members. Neuroscience researchers studied how people respond and react to the situations when other people ignore and/or reject them in a group setting. Those who were ignored or rejected by other members not only felt isolated and lonely, they also experienced headaches. There are many other clinical studies showing social isolation alone can cause a negative impact on us both psychologically and physically, such as loneliness, lack of motivation, anxiety, depression, mental breakdown, stomachaches, and headaches (Ingram & London - https://www.beyonddifferences.org/media/uploads/teacher-docs/consequences_of_social_isolation_2015-2016.pdf).

   Further, while being one of the key human needs, a good relationship has also been identified as one of the most important factors for our everyday life. In 1938, during the great depression, Harvard University initiated a longitudinal study among their 268 sophomore students to understand the key essence of a happy and healthy life. The Harvard researchers surveyed and interviewed those people every year since. More than 75 years after the start of this project, there are still 17 graduates alive (as of 2017) Interviewing those graduates as well as their spouses or significant others has revealed that a good relationship is a key ingredient for a long life. Dr. Waldinger, a director of the Harvard Study of Adult Development and a professor of psychiatrist at Harvard Medical School, said in his TED talk "Loneliness kills… good relationships don't just protect our bodies; they protect our brains." (https://news.harvard.edu/gazette/story/2017/04/over-nearly-80-years-harvard-study-has-been-showing-how-to-live-a-healthy-and-happy-life/)

2. **Respect and care** - As indicated in the study by Career System International, respect in the workplace is one of the key drivers for thriving in an organization. Another study by Harvard Medical School indicates that in a

respectful workplace, employees tend to exhibit stronger teamwork, better morale, higher job satisfaction, and fewer complaints, conflicts, and turnover (https://safnow.org/harvard-study-factors-impacting-employee-attitudes-productivity/). On the other hand, when there is a lack of respect, employees tend to show greater emotional exhaustion, conflict, and even risking companies with more grievance and lawsuits.

This is another crucial factor, not only to build employee engagement and better teamwork and productivity, but also to protect companies from the risk of increasing employees' mental illness and resulting lawsuits. So, what is the level of good relationships among members in your team? And, how are you helping your team to strengthen a culture of respect, support, and teamwork?

In addition to relationships and a caring culture in the team, leaders need to help meet more basic human needs - psychological and physiological safety.

Psychological safety - We have a need for psychological and emotional safety in our workplace to be engaged and productive. Researchers at Simon Fraser University have identified several factors that influence employees' health and performance, extensively reviewing workplace practices internationally (https://www.safety servicescompany.com/topic/workers-health/13-ways-improve-mental-health-workplace/). Psychological safety, support, and protection are some of the key factors that impact us in the workplace.

When there is psychological support, people feel and enhance their attachment to their work and organization, so they will put in more effort to perform effectively. On the other hand, if the team lacks in psychological support, it can cause the increase of absenteeism, conflicts, withdrawal behaviors, lack of productivity, accidents, and turnover.

Any forms of workplace harassment, such as power harassment, bullying, and sexual harassment are behaviors that damage psychological safety. Further, it not only affects those directly involved but also bystanders. Impacts from psychological and emotional abuse can be extensive, such as increased anxiety, stress, absenteeism, physical sickness, mental problems, problem drinking, and greater turnover, as indicated in much research.

Physiological safety and well-being — As indicated in Maslow's needs hierarchy, we want to work in a physically safe and healthy condition where break for food, drinks, and rest are available. Also, we want a good work-life balance where we can spend appropriate amount of time on personal matters, family affairs, hobbies, and personal growth, involving days off and leave. Of course, as the work-life balance is different from person to person - some people like to keep 9-to-5 work style, and some other want to work longer hours — we cannot define the right split between work and life.

In relation to a safe and reasonable work style, we want reasonable pay and benefits to maintain a quality of life. In reality, as the research indicates, pay and benefit are usually not the key reason to leave the company, unless the pay is far below the industry average or unreasonably low in relation to the amount of effort we put in.

Although work conditions may not influence people's performance in the short run, it can impact our physical health and performance in the long run. Neuroscientists' research indicates lack of sleep and rest will weaken our brain functioning. It will also negatively impact on our immune systems, so that we will become more susceptible to illness and disease, which can aggravate absenteeism and sick leave. These are the very basic human needs organizations need to meet.

So far, we have talked about what will affect members' commitment, the second factor in performance formula. In order to enhance members' commitment and engagement, the leaders need to satisfy not only the motivational factors such as meaningful work, recognition, and growth, but also more fundamental human needs to make the members work life more humane and healthy providing a connected, respectful, caring culture, and psychological safety on top of well-being and physiological safety.

Factors in Engaged Work Place

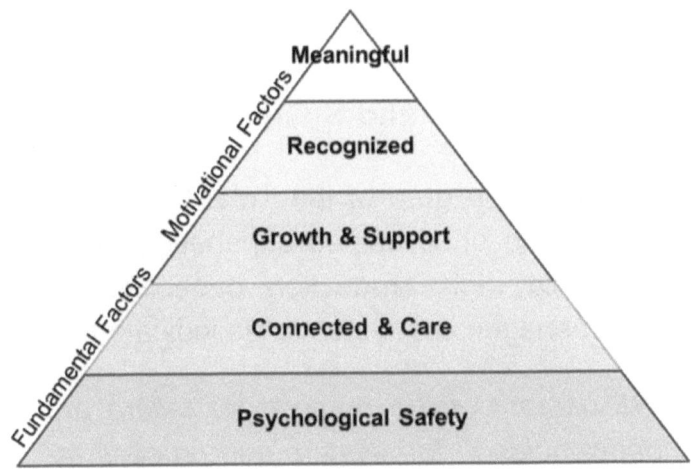

How are you ensuring psychological safety, support, and protection in your team? How is each one of your team members helping to build a psychologically safe environment for the team?

Power of Context

The third element of the performance formula is the context members are in or surrounded by. What kind of context is your team in?

Some of the contexts in the work setting are work processes, systems, policies, office environments, artifacts, and culture, in addition to the manager and colleagues. We will look into some of those factors influencing members motivation and team performance.

Work Processes and Systems

Dr. Deming is a guru of the Total Quality Management who once helped Japanese manufacturers build high production capabilities and quality management systems. He indicated:

> *"85 percent of the reasons for failure are deficiencies in the system and process rather than the employee. The role of management is to change the process rather than badgering individuals to do better."*

Back to Japanese manufacturers in 1950s. While initially focusing on identifying and eliminating defects, manufacturers in Japan moved to create processes and systems that did not produce defects in the first place. So, it's the processes and systems that help the team deliver quality performance time after time, not so much dependent on particular members' special capabilities. Good work processes and systems can prevent human errors and keep poor products and services from reaching customers and the marketplace. So, the team with robust work processes, systems, or structure can continuously deliver excellent products and services over time, without relying on a few super stars.

Work Arrangement

In the 1950s, there was research conducted by the Tavistock Institute of Human Relations in a coalfield in the UK to understand how people can work together without traditional supervisors. In this field study, groups of around 50 coalminers interchanged the various jobs while alternating shifts in ways they felt best. Output was 25 percent higher with lower costs (40 percent) than the control group (with a traditional work system with supervisors) that was similar in terms of working conditions, equipment, and the number of personnel. Accidents, sickness, and absenteeism were cut in half (Trist, Higgin, Murray and Pollock, 1963/Vol. II). Only one man left the composite faces in two years. Similar experiments with an autonomous and collaborative work system were done in other industries, such as textile and retail, and they consistently exhibited better results than a conventional work system with supervisors.

Please don't misunderstand. This is not to recommend we eliminate supervisors from the workplace. However, involving members in the planning and arranging of the work will be effective in increasing its performance and productivity.

Culture

At Economy Conference in 1996, the late Dr. Sumantra Ghoshal of the London Business School presented his stories of two comparative cultures based on his personal experiences. One culture was where people felt trust, supported, stretched, and disciplined, and the other culture was where people felt constraint, compliance, being controlled and contracted, all of which exist in many workplaces globally. He thought of this contrast when he was living and working in Fontainebleau in France, feeling refreshed in a fresh, crisp air and being happy and productive every day, versus when he was back in Kolkata in India for home leave in summer, which was very hot and super humid every day and night. (Of course, he loved Kolkata, but its summer did not allow him to work productively.)

A culture of trust, support, stretched, and disciplined versus that of constraints, compliance, controlled, and contracted - which culture do you think your members want to work in? Of course, they prefer the former, where they feel energized and engaged and do their best to accomplish their task, rather than the latter one where members feel obliged to work as they are contracted for their organization.

Dr. Schein, a former professor at the MIT Sloan School of Management, an expert in organization development from MIT, indicates workplace culture influences the behavior and mindset of members and leaders (Schein, 2004). So, the team culture, which is another variable of context, can certainly influence members' attitudes and behaviors to deliver results.

By the way, Dr. Ghoshal articulated at the conference in 1996 that it's a leader's responsibility to create organization culture. So, we can say it's a leader's responsibility to build the team culture.

In Summary

Work processes, work arrangement methods, work systems, and culture in the team have significant impacts on the members and their performance. As the Tavistock studies indicated, members get engaged, collaborative, creative, and highly productive without a supervisor when they are allowed to work autonomously and collaborate with other members in the team to identify and develop optimal work processes, systems, and policy to deliver the result. So, creating autonomous and self-directed work systems is an effective way to make the team motivated and engaged to achieve high performance.

What kind of culture does your team have? What kind of work systems does your team operate under? How much autonomy do they have to plan and do their work to achieve their mission? How much collaboration do you see in your team?

Key Concepts in Chapter 1

Performance = Competency x Commitment x Context

$\begin{Bmatrix} \text{Skills} \\ \text{knowledge} \\ \text{processes} \end{Bmatrix}$ $\begin{Bmatrix} \text{engagement} \\ \text{motivation} \\ \text{confidence} \end{Bmatrix}$ $\begin{Bmatrix} \text{members/relationship} \\ \text{work processes/systems} \\ \text{team culture} \end{Bmatrix}$

Engagement Factors

a) Motivational factors $\begin{Bmatrix} \text{Meaningfulness} \\ \text{Recognized} \\ \text{Supported \& growth} \end{Bmatrix}$

b) Fundamental factors $\begin{Bmatrix} \text{Connected \& care} \\ \text{Psychological \& physiological} \\ \text{safety} \end{Bmatrix}$

Principles of Engaged and Productive Teams:

#1: *"Create a strong meaning in work"*

#2: *"Enhance members' competency through developmental support"*

#3: *"Build a connected and caring team culture."*

#4: *"Build an autonomous and self-directed culture."*

#5: *"Build highly productive work systems and environment."*

Chapter 2

Key Success Factors of High-Performance Teams

Framework of Highly Effective Teams

Why can high-performance teams continuously deliver great results? High-performance teams must have something in common to make them great. In this Chapter, we will review some of the key frameworks and success factors of highly effective teams.

You will have personally experienced several teams in your life, including during your school days. Some teams are good or great, and others are not so good. Pick the best team you have experienced that had great teamwork and also achieved good results collaboratively. What are some of the key success factors for that team?

When I ask this question to managers, I always get a wide variety of responses. Nonetheless, when probing them for priority elements, they usually respond that key elements of effective teams are aligned goal or direction, strong, effective leaders, open communication, good relationship and competent members.

LaFasto and Larson (2001) studied real-life teams and indicated that the five critical factors that ensure the teams' success are (a) collaborative and open relationships in the team, (b) effective problem-solving processes, (c) members' ability and behaviors to maximize team results, (d) effective team leaders who can guide the team toward its success, and (e) an organizational environment that enhances effective teamwork, such as team systems, processes, policies, etc.

Effective team leaders and competent members are the keys to a high-performance team. Their research also confirmed the importance of establishing a productive environment, including the system, process, structure, and policy. Further, collaborative and open relationships are also important, as they are fundamental human requirements to work humanly and productively.

Patrick Lencioni (2011), in his book titled *Five Dysfunctions of Teams*, articulates the importance of trust in the team, based on his research on dysfunctional teams. Members in dysfunctional teams cannot build trust, as they are fearful of becoming vulnerable to other members. As they do not trust other members, they feel fear of conflict and do not debate with other members. As they do not articulate their own ideas and opinions, they don't feel accountable for team results. As they are not accountable, they lack attention to team projects. As no one is attending to team projects, the team cannot attain its goal. So, trust is one of the team's foundations that facilitates active communication and collaboration in the team.

Researchers indicated that communication has positive influences on team performance and efficient team process (Mathieu, Heffner, Goodwin, Salas, & Cannon-Bowers, 2000; Zaccaro, Rittman and Marks, 2001). Communication quality actually influences the team performance. While LaFasto and Larson put "communication" as part of "problem-solving," we will include it as one of key ingredients for a high-performance team.

Katzenbach and Smith (2005) articulate that the team purpose and goals are must-have elements for high-performance teams, as they will drive members' shared commitment and laser-like focus. The importance of direction, such as the purpose and goals, is also indicated in LaFasto and Larson's study as part of an organizational environment having a clear direction.

Reflecting above research findings, key framework or essential factors of effective teams are as follows:

1) Direction that is clear and meaningful
2) Leadership/membership who are competent
3) Roles that are clear
4) Systems that enhance productivity and collaboration
5) Communication that is open and constructive
6) Trusting relationship

Please see the "Team Effectiveness Framework" in below graphic.

Framework for Effective Team

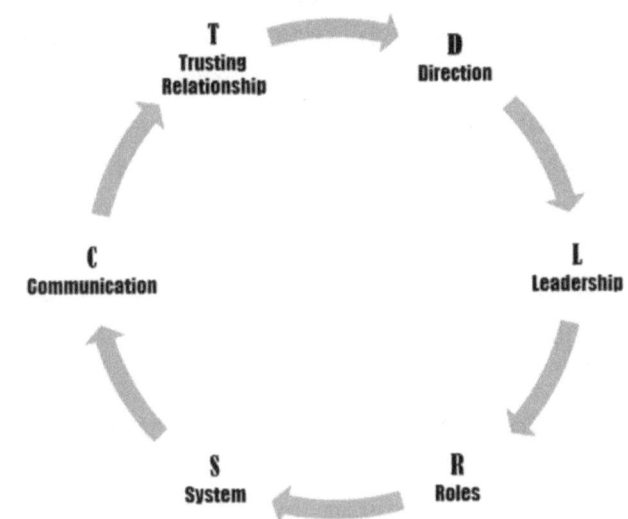

The important responsibilities of managers and team leaders are to build those team effectiveness factors in place, to increase the team performance and success rate. Leaders also need to make sure that their team members understand the fundamental framework of effective teams, so that they are mindful of those elements and collaborate to build those frameworks to continuously achieve team goals.

I have been helping hundreds of teams in various industries enhance their team effectiveness by facilitating them to identify their strengths and improvement areas of their team effectiveness factors. As a result of the workshops, they collaboratively act on their improvement plans for some of those six factors and enhance their productivity. Their improvement areas can be different. However, many of those who have issues in collaboration, don't have trusting relationships or aligned directions.

I will discuss those essential factors in detail in the next section.

Direction - That Is Clear and Meaningful

All teams have some sort of direction, such as goals, a revenue target, projects, key performance indicators, target completion dates, and so on and so forth, and yet, some are performing great, and some others are not. Why?

Goal Clarity

A clear goal plays an important role in aligning members toward achieving a common goal. Research suggests that teams often fail because they are given a vague goals and tasks (Hackman, 1990), or because leaders or members replace the team goal with a personal agenda or other interests (Larson & LaFasto, 1989). A clear direction and focus on priority need to be two key management practices (Larson & LaFasto, 2001).

Further, research indicates that group members working toward a specific, challenging goal tend to work harder than group members without an explicit performance goal (Weingart & Weldon, 1991). This is consistent with the previously introduced data indicating "challenging and meaningful work is a key motivational factor." The level of goals also has a strong impact on both the group process and performance (Weldon, Jehn, & Pradhan, 1991).

Having aligned goals is especially important for cross-functional teams, as each one of the members may likely have separate goals and values from their own function. Thus, team leaders need to ensure a clear direction and specific, challenging goals for all the team members.

Meaningful Mission

Great teams have a clear mission or reason for being or why they exist. It's certainly not revenue or profit. The team mission needs to be related with and contributing to its stakeholders and community. Members are looking for meaning in their work. Or, said differently, the more meaning members identify with the work, the more pride and engagement they feel with their work and team.

The mission is the north, indicating why we are doing what we are doing, and what we should be focusing on to get there. A well-crafted mission can, not only enhance members' engagement but also unite all members' minds toward achieving it. It helps the team to collaborate voluntarily without being told by the leader, because they know what values they need to achieve as a team, collaborating with other members.

Inspiring Vision

Along with the meaningful mission, the vision will give clarity for what the team is striving to achieve in the future, or what kind of world they are creating in the long run. While a mission statement tells why the team exists, vision indicates what the team aspires to be. So, the vision is the future state of desired world the team is creating. Vision needs to be meaningful, inspiring, vivid, and clear, so that team members feel motivated and inspired to continuously work to achieve its vision. It may be important to note that while the mission is long-term, the vision can change or expand as the environment and team's scope and competency changes.

Team Values

Team values are an important guide for leaders and members to make the right choice when they make a decision on encountering a fork in the road. The team values also play an important role in building the right mindset, behaviors, and habits for members to consistently work together effectively as a team. For instance, if the team wants highly engaged members, we must value people, and so, many teams have "people" as one of the team's values. Or, if we want lots of innovation in the team, we must value innovative behaviors. So, there needs to be "innovation" as part of the team values.

Team Strategy / Key Focus

The final element of the direction is team strategy or key focus. While each member has their own roles and responsibilities, knowing the overarching core team strategy will guide team members to collaborate and coordinate to achieve the common goal of the team. Please note that strategy is not a shopping list of activities. It's a focused set of actions. A good strategy gives members a clear focus.

How clear and inspiring are your team's mission, vision, values, and strategic focuses to your members? Also, how clearly do your stakeholders understand your team's directions?

Effective Leadership

I've seen many strong leaders in the last several decades, but not all of their teams are high performing. What separates great teams from not so great teams? Where do we see leadership in really high performing teams? Where do you see leadership in your team?

High-performance teams have an excellent leader at the top, and each member of the team also exhibits solid leadership in their own responsible areas, which makes the team really high performing.

Creating an inspiring direction may not work if the leader doesn't live the mission, vision, and values. "Effective leadership processes represent perhaps the most important factor in the success of organizational team" (Zaccaro et al., 2001). The top leader ensures all members understand and are fully on board to live the team values, as this is vital to build teamwork. At the same time, the leader orchestrates the team to effectively accomplish the team mission to achieve its vision, and navigates the team when encountering heavy storms, such as unexpected new challenges from the market and competitors or unreasonable requests from other functions or senior executives.

"Effective leaders need to take all necessary actions, whether internally or externally, in a systematic way to build several important systems and capabilities to lead their teams to success. Strong leaders need to be behaviorally flexible and have a wide repertoire of skills to meet the diverse needs of the team" (Barge, 1996). This indicates that leaders need to continually assess and improve their leadership capability in order to guide the team to success time after time.

Leadership Everywhere in the Team

In addition to the effective leader at the top, each member of the high-performance team is fully committed and takes a lead to deliver their accountable results. They know what's required to make things happen. They are also eager to upgrade their skill set to stay as an expert in their responsible area and exhibit professionalism.

As indicated by Center for Creative Leadership, we need leadership at every level of an organization. Likewise, we see leadership from all members in high-performance teams. The team leader supports and orchestrates the team, when necessary, to effectively maximize the team results.

So, how do you lead your team? And, how do your members lead their own projects to lead the team's success? We will review leadership quality and actions in the following Chapter.

Clearly Defined Roles

There are several roles in the team that can execute the strategy and achieve the team mission. What are the key roles and responsibilities in your team? How are those roles allocated to each member of your team? How are the roles determined? And, how were they delegated?

Typical problems found in many teams are (1) narrowly defined roles and responsibilities, (2) misaligned roles and responsibilities among the team members and (3) wrongly allocated resources.

First, members working based on narrowly defined roles, job descriptions or manuals that indicate detailed tasks and activities may be ok when stakeholders' needs and practices remain the same from the time those manuals are made. However, in today's fast-changing world, customers and stakeholders' demands and habits change from time to time. So, narrowly defined roles and responsibilities can hinder the team in best meeting stakeholders' changing needs and concerns.

Roles and responsibilities must be determined based on the team mission and strategy. So, it should indicate accountability or expected results from the role, rather than its tasks and activities. Suppose you are the brand manager of product X with the mission of maximizing branding. What could be your roles? Your roles could be (1) branding or building brand image and equity, and (2) building your members and team's capabilities. It's not just upgrading current products and services, nor creating advertising campaigns and promotions. And, the responsibilities will be modified or changed when the strategy is modified or changed. For example, in this internet world, branding will also be done through Social Network Systems (SNS), rather than traditional TV commercial or other types of mass media. So, it's wise to shift from activity-focused roles and responsibilities to accountability-focused ones.

Second, misaligned roles and responsibilities among the team members - I have often observed this tendency in unproductive or uncooperative teams, where members only know their roles and responsibilities but do not know specifically what other members are doing, or they know only vaguely. There are some challenges in this type of team: (1) they work independently and do not collaborate, so there is not much synergy in the team, (2) some members are doing overlapping and redundant work, and (3) when receiving and responding to requests from stakeholders about something they are not familiar with, they pass the stakeholder request to other team members, or they spend lots of time arguing and deciding who is responsible for handling that case within the team, which can create frustrated customers.

In a high performing team, each member not only understands their roles and responsibilities, but also those of other members. Also, they understand how they coordinate and support each other when the team receives new or unfamiliar requests or challenges from their stakeholders. They also know how to back each other up when other members are taking a day-off. Aligned roles and responsibilities are keys to creating synergy and optimizing a positive customer experience.

Third, misallocated resources are a common issue in many teams. I often hear from managers that they have some members who are hard workers and do lots of tasks even working overtime, and some others that are slow and take on a limited amount of work. As everyone initially joins the team with different experiences and capabilities, allocating the roles based on the capacity of each team member is fine. However, it should not create inequality of work effort and time among the team. This can cause complaints from the hard workers about those who are not working effectively and efficiently, or complaints from those who work slow and less, saying that they are not well taken care of by the manager or the team.

In a high performing team, the roles are allocated in a way that requires each and every member to do the best to accomplish their role. This will help the team grow and keep work disciplined, and a healthy atmosphere within the team.

Well-defined, aligned, and allocated roles and responsibilities are essential for the team to function at a higher level, collaborate, and grow as one team. It may be worthwhile for you to review (1) how the roles and responsibilities are defined, (2) how those roles and responsibilities are understood and aligned among the team members, and (3) how fairly those roles are allocated among the team.

Work System Matters

Results-driven and enabling a work system and environment is necessary for teams to deliver results effectively and efficiently (Hackman &

Walton, 1986; Larson & LaFasto, 1989, LaFasto & Larson, 2001). That could be one of the key initiatives leaders can take. Where should you start to make a better change?

LaFasto & Larson (2001) indicated that "important factors for team success are (1) effective management practices that set the direction, align plans, and deliver results, (2) team structure and processes that ensure the best decisions are made as quickly as possible by the right people, and (3) systems that provide useful information and drive behavior toward desired results" (p. 161). Further, those elements need to fit together to consistently generate the right behaviors of team members individually and collectively to achieve a common goal as a team (Hanna, 1988; LaFasto & Larson, 2001). So, some of the key factors are "goal-setting and planning processes," "work processes and structures with effective decision-making systems," and "information sharing systems."

High-Performance Work System

There are a lot of systems that promote or hinder the team performance and productivity. Suppose you are leading a bakery team producing bread for the restaurant. What systems do you need to build?

One of the key systems in a bakery team is a supply chain system, from ordering ingredients to producing bread to quality checking to packing to delivering it to the restaurant. What else do we need? Before producing, we may need planning and aligning with the restaurant around the type and quantity of the bread to deliver. How about people processes, such as recruiting and hiring a new staff, giving an orientation, training and developing members?

Good work processes and systems will connect members and help them share needed information and collaborate to deliver their common goal. Poor processes and systems will divide and keep the team from working together. High-performance teams have both business and people systems in place.

What kind of systems and structure does your team have to help the team produce high-quality results year in and year out? And, how are those systems congruent with the team mission and values, and how are they interrelated, interdependent, and integrative with other systems to achieve the organization's mission and values.

In a later chapter, we will review what kind of systems, processes, or structure team leaders need to strengthen or create to consistently deliver high-quality products and services to the stakeholders - such as planning and decision-making systems, team processes, information sharing, and member and team development systems.

Communication Matters

How well do you communicate with your team members? Do you find yourself communicating more with some members than others? If you do, what difference does that create in terms of the amount of information and ideas you receive from the members? Also, what are those differences in your communication amount from member to member impacting the relationship between you and members? Lastly, how is that difference impacting your team performance?

Communication in the team is just like the nervous system that transmits signals among various parts of our body to coordinate actions to live healthily or normally. So, if there is a problem in our nervous system, our body cannot communicate and coordinate well, our body will not be able to function well. Communication is a vital factor for the team to function well and produce good results. Research also suggests that effective communication is one of the key factors in making better decisions (McGrath, 1984).

Some of the communication problems I often hear from managers are as follows:

1. I am not getting all the information I need from my team.
2. Some members are not sharing information proactively in the team.
3. Many members use emails and texting to communicate with members, even when they can talk face-to-face.
4. Some members don't voice their opinions and ideas in the team meeting.
5. I don't receive important information fast enough.
6. Bad news often comes in late.

Have you had any issues like the above?

Conversely, problems I often hear from team members are the followings:

1. I don't have the information I need to do my work.

2. I am not getting all the information I need from my manager.
3. I seldom receive feedback from my manager.
4. I cannot share information that is conflicting with that from my manager.
5. I don't want to voice my opinion in the team.

Members in high-performance teams communicate openly and transparently. They not only share important data timely, but also voice their ideas, opinions, and feelings and give critiques to the team without much worry. That's why they can identify issues before they become problems most of the time. If a problem occurs, solve it effectively, and produce innovation from time to time. Open and effective communication is truly needed to be high performing.

So, how well do your team members communicate with each other to share thoughts and information to plan, decide, implement, and coordinate to deliver the desired results? If it's not superb, what are the improvement areas in communication in your team? What is causing those communication challenges? Then, what can you do as a leader to make the team communication work to enhance your team performance?

We will later review how leaders can enhance team communication both in terms of quality and quantity to deliver high performance.

Trusting Relationship

As revealed by the longitudinal study by Harvard University introduced in Chapter 1, having a good relationship is the fundamental human need to live and work healthily and happily. Good teamwork is built on good relationships among the team members. Good relationships will result in good communication among the team members, and increased communication will further strengthen relationships, which will accelerate collaboration within the team.

Collaborative relationships with co-workers are an important factor for members to engage with their teams and organizations (Kaye & Jordan-Evans, 2005). Engagement of the member is not just built on their work-related motivation, but also on a good, collaborative relationship with colleagues. So, leaders need to build collaborative team relationships to increase its team effectiveness (Zaccaro et al., 2001; Kozlowski and Ilgen. 2006).

To build healthy relationships in the team, there needs to be the psychological safety where people feel safe about being there and sharing their opinions and ideas. That's the baseline. On top of the psychological safety, members need respect and care. Then, the members also want to be recognized, appreciated, and supported to feel positive and engaged in the team.

Trust Factors

To be truly collaborative, we need to build trust in the team beyond good relationships. There are lots of benefits of building trust in the team. With trust, members share their concerns and problems with other members quickly, which will help the team tackle and solve the issues fast. With trust, the members openly share their ideas. However, they may be unpopular and Out-of-the-box?, which can result in innovative products, services, or processes to achieve better performance.

Who do you trust most in your team? Who is the most trustworthy person for you in the organization? How are they different from those who are not as trustworthy? Charley Green, the co-author of *Trusted Adviser*, stresses the importance of four factors impacting trustworthiness, i.e., credibility, reliability, intimacy, and self-orientation (Green & Howe, 2012). Although the book appears to focus on buyer-seller situations, it's worthwhile understanding the basic concept of "trust equation."

In the trust equation, credibility is about one's knowledge, skills, and experiences, so that we feel the people are credible to work together. Reliability is about one's achievements that are consistently delivered, so we feel we can rely on this person. Intimacy is about psychological safety and a feeling of closeness, so that we feel like continuing a long-term relationship. While those three factors are trust-building factors, self-orientation is a subtracting or dividing factor. As the word indicates, self-orientation is how much he or she is focused on themselves or their own benefits rather than that of the other party. So, even though one has a solid credibility, reliability, and intimacy, he or she may not be trustworthy if their self-orientation is too strong.

Trustworthiness is certainly an important factor, so you may want to check your trustworthiness level against those four factors from your members' point of views - how would they feel about your credibility, reliability, intimacy, and self-orientation as a leader. What are your strengths? Which ones are your improvement opportunities?

Further, we must build trust in the entire team, not just among key members. As often emphasized in Total Quality Management Principles, "The strength of the chain is determined by the weakest link." So, if there is mistrust or poor relationships in the team, we likely miss some important information or ideas in our planning and execution of the decision, so we may not perform our best; or worse yet, deliver unsatisfactory products and services to our stakeholders.

Finally, a trusting relationship has been crucial, especially for cross-functional teams to effectively deliver expected results, in the presence of the challenges that those team members who must work together have different goals and values from their own functions, work on multiple teams simultaneously, and report to multiple leaders, e.g., their functional manager and team leaders (Webber, 2002).

What is the trust level among the members in your team? How do you measure the level of trust?

We can't buy trust, and we need to earn trust over time. While we cannot build trust overnight, there are many ways we can build and earn trust. We will review leadership actions to build trusting relationships in the team in the later chapters on "Leadership Actions."

In Summary

Highly effective teams have the following essential factors.

1) Aligned Direction: The team mission, vision, values, and strategic focuses are inspiring, clearly defined, understood, and aligned among the team. This aligned direction is the key to building a vector in the team.
2) Effective Leadership: The team leader effectively orchestrates members toward achieving the vision. All the members are

capable and passionate about performing their roles with strong ownership.

3) **Clear Roles:** Everyone in the team is very clear about their roles and responsibilities. They also understand other member's roles, and how to support, coordinate, and collaborate to achieve the team goals, even when some members are missing.

4) **Robust Systems:** Highly effective teams have robust work processes and systems to help the team work effectively and are continuously evolving its team effectiveness to enhance productivity and collaboration. It deals with both work process/systems and human development systems.

5) **Open and Constructive Communication:** Effective communication is the blood of the team effectiveness as it fuels critical data and information for the teamwork as well as the energy for the team relationships. The robust systems' effectiveness depends on the level of communication in the team.

6) **Trusting Relationship:** At one end of effective communication, there are good relationships in the team, which bond all the members into a unity. With trust, mem-

bers communicate and work very honestly without worries.

As a leader, we need to understand where we are in the journey of building a high performing team in terms of the above six factors. Which factors are your team's strengths, and which elements have need of further development? What actions do you want to take to move forward to reach your team destination?

Please take the below survey to preliminarily assess the strengths and improvement areas in terms of your team effectiveness factors on a 5-point scale; with 5 being excellent and 1 being poor. Then, please place the average score of each of the 6 dimensions on the radar chart on the following page.

	Team Effectiveness Survey Items (a short version)	Rating
1	The purpose, mission, vision, and specific goals of our team are clear and we all understand them.	
2	We all understand our team's strategy, plans, and success measures to achieve the goals.	
3	Our roles and goals are clearly defined, and we are all committed to achieving those.	

4	We understand the roles and responsibilities of other members and how to coordinate and support each other.	
5	We have established processes, systems, and methodologies to decide and implement the strategy, plans, and tasks.	
6	Our meetings are effective to identify and solve problems, make decisions, and improve our plans and goals collaboratively.	
7	We never avoid difficult issues; we discuss them constructively.	
8	We openly and timely share with other members our opinions and feedback in a way they understand us.	
9	We all respect, support, and praise each other to help us grow and succeed.	
10	When there are mistakes, we do not blame anyone, but rather, we collaborate to achieve our common objective.	
11	We all clearly understand and exhibit expected behaviors in the team with pride.	
12	Good work is always recognized, and we all feel motivated with a sense of accomplishment.	
13	We collaboratively move our projects and tasks as scheduled, and we continually accomplish our goals.	
14	We are a great team, and all are satisfied with working and contributing in this team.	

Q1-2: Direction; Q3-4: Roles; Q5-6: Systems; Q7-8: Communication;

Q9-10: Trusting relationship; Q11-12: Leadership; Q13-14: Results

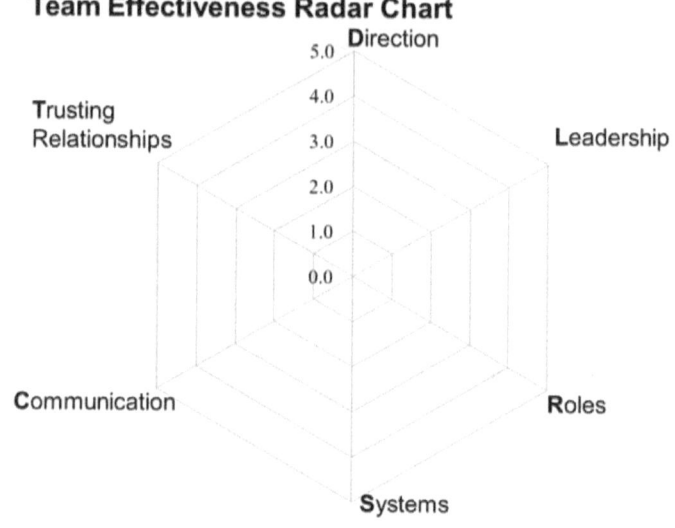

CHAPTER 3

LEADERSHIP MATTERS

Leaders' Mission and Roles

Who are your ideal leaders with whom you worked with or even just heard about, regardless of industries or fields including sports, science, and politics? Why do you think those leaders are ideal or great? What have they achieved?

Marriam-Webster dictionary defines leadership as "act of leading" and "capacity to lead." Peter Northouse (2005), the author of *Leadership: Theory and Practices*, defines leadership as "a process whereby an individual influences a group of individuals to achieve a common goal."

Going back to my above questions, I believe your ideal leaders have achieved something that is beneficial for the team, organization, community, or even country. What important legacy have they left that has long-lasting impacts on their organization or in their field?

In order to continuously attain a common goal, leaders have 3 types of roles and deliverables:

(1) mission or business goal achievement,
(2) people development, and
(3) organization development.

Good leaders make a difference to their business or progress toward its mission. Further, great leaders build both people and teams or organizational capability, as they are the power engines to continuously deliver great results time after time.

How are you currently performing those three roles as a leader? What, specifically, have you delivered in business/mission achievement, member development, and team development in the last 12 months? How do you measure your progress in those areas?

Business Development / Mission Achievement

We can measure their business development by their business accomplishments against targets. Based on our survey, more than two-thirds of leaders say they do fairly good job in this area. Why? Because attaining business goals or increasing revenues are the top priorities for most companies and organizations. So, the manager's results and contributions are being measured by their business development or mission attainment. Naturally, the managers placed key attention on the revenue growth or goal achievement, and their key topic of conversation with members is about work results and numbers to ensure all members are focusing on delivering their results for the team.

People Development. How do you measure the progress of your members? Some organizations measure members' progress based on their performance progress – how much they have achieved on their assigned tasks versus the previous year or against the goals – output quantity, its quality and the speed of completion.

Other organizations are also measuring the people development by checking how members have grown their professional capability, such as technical skills and knowledge, over a period of time, using competency models and performance measurement.

Our survey indicates less than half of the leaders feel confident in developing their people as they would like. Many indicate they don't have time to give feedback or coach their members as their organization expects more with less time in this fast-changing world. Some do not even have a list of target skill sets to measure members' competency levels. Why? While many organizations say, "people are our key asset, or even the most important asset," the reality is not quite so. In many organizations, executives and senior leaders do not coach and teach their people; it is often the case that they don't feel responsible for training and developing their direct reports. In such organizations, managers think training is an HR department's responsibility, and development is the individuals' responsibility.

In high performing organizations, leaders from the top of the organization do develop their members by offering feedback and coaching to their members. Executives and senior leaders run classes and courses to develop managers and employees. An example of this would be General Electric offering a wide variety of development programs both at the Crotonville Leadership Center in New York where the CEO and executives teach. Most people learn best when working with a boss who is passionate about developing their members; learner-friendly programs, systems, and culture will help. Leaders are the driver for a learning culture.

Team development. The third leadership role is team development. How is team development different from people development? While people development is about building individuals' capability and capacity, team development is about building engaging and productive team cultures. For example, suppose you own a good sport team and get many good players while paying lots of contract fees. But your team are not winning as much as you would like. What is the problem? Most likely, your team isn't playing as a team. Teams can be effective if there is teamwork built on trust among the members and collaboration skills and systems – not just the excellent skills of a handful members. How do you measure leaders' effectiveness in team development? You can measure it two ways; (1) improved levels of trust among the team, and (2) productivity improvement achieved through improving processes, systems, and environment.

In my team leadership workshops, I ask participants to rate their performance as to how well they perform those three roles and deliverables on a 5-point scale, with 5 being excellent. They almost always rate their business development results the highest; and their second-highest rating goes to people development. The lowest rating is for organization development, which is usually 3 or below. As most managers were promoted to the management and supervising position because of their business development capability, many of them have not been trained in how to grow and develop members or teams.

If we want our team to perform well long-term, we, as leaders, need to develop all the three areas - business, people, and teams.

It's all about the intention of leaders that influences their actions and performance in the three responsible areas. An intention creates attention, attention generates actions and behaviors, and those actions and behaviors produce outcomes. If the leader's focus is solely on business results, then most of their actions are about delivering business outcomes. To be a high-performance team leader, leaders need to have an intention to develop business, members, and teams in a balanced manner.

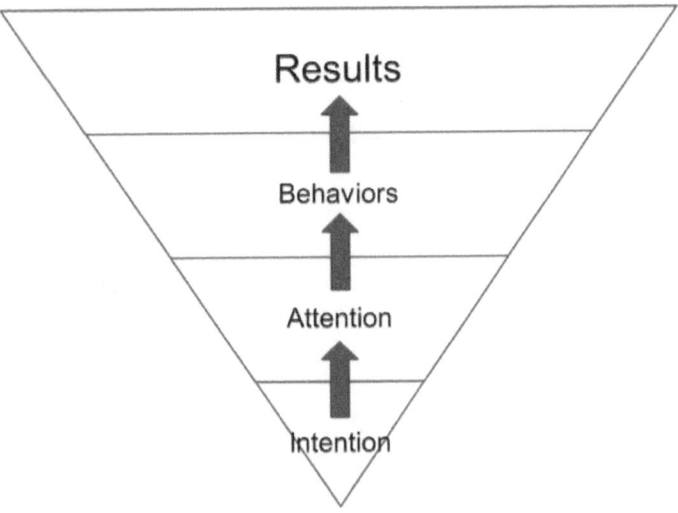

So, where is your focused intention among those three roles and outcomes as a leader? which roles are you currently focusing on and performing well? Do you have a balanced intention and attention to those three areas?

Reflecting on your self-assessment, what will be your new goals for each responsible area? Then, what actions do you want to take to start building a high-performance team?

Leader's 3 Roles:

Build Business x Grow Member x Develop Team

Impact of Leadership

In Chapter 1, we discussed:

> Performance = Competency x Commitment x Context
>
> Engagement drives the productivity.
>
> Key motivators for members are "meaningful work," "supportive boss," "recognition," and "personal and professional growth."

What is that data indicating to us?

It indicates that leaders are in the best position to influence members' engagement and commitment to improve team performance and results. For example, first, leaders can assign their members to meaningful and challenging work. Poor leaders just tell members what roles to play or what tasks to perform, without mentioning why it's important, or how the task is related to a larger team or organizational goal. Good leaders help members identify the meaning in their work through coaching conversation.

Second, leaders can build members' engagement by fully respecting them, engaging in a quality conversation with them, and supporting them to help achieve their goals. They recognize good work and meet members' needs for self-esteem. Poor leaders are not much interested in talking with members nor supporting members to develop and achieve their success. Good leaders are fully committed to helping members succeed.

Third, leaders can fulfill members' sense of growth and accomplishment through coaching and education whenever needed and appropriate. Poor leaders think learning and development as either an HR responsibility or the member's responsibility. So, they don't offer members any coaching and learning opportunities. Good leaders are fully committed to helping members grow and succeed, and giving encouragement, feedback, and coaching.

Research done by Career System International also identified managers as a key reason for employees leaving a company - those who don't offer the above support for their members can demotivate their members, demoralize the team, lower the team performance, and worse, keep having demotivated and actively disengaged members in the team who may further worsen the team morale. Soon or later, they will likely lose good members in addition to gaining disengaged members. No wonder many HR professionals say that people join the company (for its attractiveness) and leave the manager (owing to their poor attitudes and interpersonal skills). So, in your current leadership practices, which type of actions are you doing more – actions to activate members' engagement and performance or those discouraging members to engage and grow?

Further, *Gallup* indicates that managers are accountable for at least 70% of the variance in employee engagement scores across business units (https://news.gallup.com/businessjournal/182792/managers-account-variance-employee-engagement.aspx).

In summary, although we often hear that poor employee engagement is created by poor work policies, conditions, pay, and also frequent changes in organizations, bosses or leaders are the key influencer and can significantly improve team's engagement, motivation, performance, and productivity. Now, here's a question for you.

How can you strengthen your team's engagement and performance?

I will discuss what leaders or managers can do to positively impact the team motivation and performance in a later Chapter, so you can determine specific action plans to make it happen within 3 to 6 months.

Leadership Versus Management Approaches

Current leaders need to practice both managerial and leadership approaches and actions in a balanced manner. In many organizations, especially where employee engagement is low, managers are using a managerial approach predominantly. Understanding the differences between management and leadership will be very helpful for us to determine what actions we should take as a leader. How is leadership and management different for you? Or do you use them interchangeably?

A managerial approach is effective in maintaining and improving current performance and operations to achieve maximum efficiency. In the late1800s, Henri Fayol, a French management guru, articulated the importance of five managerial actions - planning, organizing, commanding, coordinating, and controlling to efficiently achieve its goals, based on his experience as both an engineer and the Managing Director of a mining company. These administrative actions are still important in our current organizations. Fast-forward 100+ years, Dr. Kotter, the professor of leadership at Harvard Business School suggests there are three kinds of key managerial actions - performance management, organizing, and problem-solving.

1. **Manage performance** - This includes effective goal-setting, planning, implementation, and progress review until accomplishment. It's mostly actions around the performance management cycle.
2. **Organizing** – This has a range of activities, such as structuring and allocating necessary resources (people, budget, external resources, information, policy, and system) to achieve the organization's mission.
3. **Problem-Solving** - When identifying problems, managers need to solve them. Also, when finding improvement opportu-

nities, they will make improvements to efficiently achieve their goals.

Many managers usually do these 3 kinds of actions well, as achieving goals is a key reason they were promoted to a management position. These managerial actions have primarily remained the same for more than 100 years (since the Industrial Revolution, which built a command-and-control hierarchical culture in the organization). However, in this fast-changing economy, this capability alone is not enough to grow the team.

As Dr. Marshall Goldsmith, one of the world-renowned executive coaches, articulated, "What got you here will not get you there," meaning skill sets you used at the current position will not be sufficient at the next level, so you must be prepared if you want to step up. Specifically, present leaders or managers need to practice an effective leadership approach more. A leadership approach helps organizations move toward a new vision or world, in contrast with managerial maintenance actions in a given framework. Therefore, when we talk about leadership, we also talk about their vision, and leaders without vision are hopeless and not inspiring to an organization's members.

There are still more organizations with a command-and-control type management culture compared to those with more inspiring leadership culture. Also, there are many teams that have a command-and-control culture. Beyond managing the team effectively, what do leaders need to focus on to enhance members' motivation and engagement? Dr. Kotter indicates, although both are important, leadership and management are extremely different: management (managerial actions) produces efficiency in the current system, and leadership promotes changes toward achieving the vision to take the organization to the future. He suggests the top 3 actions in leadership are as follows:

1. **Create a vision** – As the leader is taking the organization to the future, she or he needs to create the future vision – a better world or the desired state of the organization in the future.
2. **Align people** – Then, the leader needs to communicate the vision, gain people's buy-in, and align their minds to walking toward the ideal organization vision. The

alignment among the members is the key to create synergistic power in the organization.
3. **Motivate and inspire** – The leader motivates and energizes people to take needed actions to move and co-create the future vision. So, it's leaders' magnetic power that makes people follow, not command and order.

When I ask the group of managers as to which actions they take more, management versus leadership, more often than not, the majority of their responses are "management" actions. We need to take both leadership and managerial actions in a balanced manner to effectively lead the team to deliver optimal performance. The management and leadership ratio will be different depending on the state of the team and its business and environment. When the business is stagnant and customer needs, competitors' strategies, and environments are changing, the leader needs to take leadership actions to improve the business and team. And, after implementing the major change initiatives, the leader may gradually shift the energy toward management actions to build stability and efficiency in the team.

Leadership vs Management

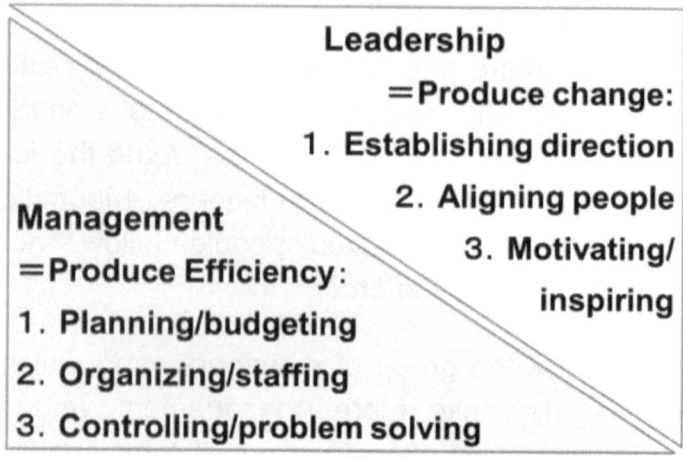

(by Dr. John P. Kotter)

What would be the optimal balance between leadership and management for your team management based on your current business situation? What leadership and management actions do you need to take to optimize your team's performance? And what actions do you need to reduce to tackle bigger tickets and high priority issues?

5 Key Leaders Actions

So far, we reviewed the leader's mission, three roles, and two approaches to performing as a leader. How well do you usually complete the three roles and deliverables of leaders? How balanced is your intention, attention, and actions for building the business, people, and your team? Where do you want to shift your attention and actions moving forward to take your team performance to the next level?

Now I like to introduce you to the five key actions to build a highly engaged and productive team. Do you still remember the key issues members are experiencing, and the important factors that can build their engagement in the workplace? How about the team performance principles?

Yes, one of the major problems in many organizations is poor employee engagement. Key factors to enhance members' engagement are "meaningful work," "recognition, care, and support," "personal and professional growth," and "relationship." "Autonomous work arrangement," and "effective work processes and systems" can also help members engage, increase productivity, and build a high performing culture in the workplace. To address those opportunities, there are five team performance principles leaders should be aware of and act on. Let's briefly check those five principles in the below chart.

Team Performance Principles:

#1: "Create a strong meaning at work" as members are looking for meaningful and challenging work. This also help members feel a sense of contribution and self-worth.

#2: "Enhance members' competency through developmental support" as members want to grow as a person and also as a professional, which will also be a base for their promotion. This will also increase their market value.

#3: "Build a connected and caring team culture" as this is a basic human need not only to stay psychologically and emotionally healthy but also to increase the quality and speed of communication and collaboration.

#4: "Build an autonomous and self-directed culture" as this can make members motivated, more creative, and collaborative, which results in higher productivity.

#5: "Build highly productive work systems and environment" as aligned work processes and systems can significantly increase productivity and reduce defects and safety problems.

There are five key leadership actions to act upon the above five key team performance principles. They are to engage, envision, empower, enable and establish.

1) **Engage** - For creating a trusting and collaborative team, a leader first needs to engage and trust their members and build a trusting community in their team where all members in the team communicate openly and support each other to achieve their common goals. Secondly, the leader needs to trust and collaborate with their peers in the related functions across the organization. High-performance teams have a trusting and collaborative leader, and members who truly respect and trust each other work together effectively.

2) **Envision** - Leaders need to show the clear, inspiring future state of their teams, so that members are clear about where

they are going, why they are moving toward that direction, and what they are doing.

3) **Empower** - Leaders, not only engage all members toward a common goal, but also motivate and energize members to act on translating the team vision into strategic actions and implementing them to achieve the goals.

4) **Enable Members** - Through a variety of development methods, leaders need to help members grow personally and professionally and build the competency to be able to perform their tasks.

5) **Enhance Systems and Environment** - Leaders need to enhance and enable work processes, systems, structure, and environment to make teams productive, collaborative, efficient, and risk-free.

See the below chart indicating how those five leadership actions will help address the members' needs while building the key factors of effective teams.

Relationship between "member needs," "leadership actions," and the "6 factors of the team."

Members Five Needs	Five Leadership Actions	6 Factors of the Team					
		D	L	R	S	C	T
Psycho. Safety	Engage					√	√
Meaning	Envision	√	√				
Autonomy	Empower		√	√			√
Growth	Enable Members		√	√	√		
Productive Env	Enhance System				√	√	√

D=Direction, **L**=Leadership, **R**=Roles, **S**=Systems, **C**=Communication, **T**=Trusting relationship

In Summary

Leaders have a significant impact on building members' engagement, addressing members' needs for meaningful work, recognition, support, and a healthy working environment. While poor leaders create actively disengaged members and increased turnover, effective leaders build commitment in members to excel in their performance.

To be an effective team leader, we need to have a balanced focus (intention and attention) on three roles, i.e., business, members, and team development. Leaders with balanced intention and actions will be able to continuously achieve high-performance results, as they produce not only business results, but also enhancing members' capacity and system capability. On the contrary, those who only focus on business achievements may reduce and lose the capacity of members and their team's system.

To successfully achieve a leader's three roles, we should be able to perform both management and leadership approaches. Management or managerial actions are effective in improving the efficiency in the team. So, when the team is suffering from inefficiencies in their work, such as two members working on similar tasks and doing overlapping and redundant work, the leader needs to help the members identify ways to eliminate those inefficient work practices and systems to increase efficiency.

In contrast, leadership produces changes toward the new team vision or ideal future team state. So, when the team performance stalls due to the customer expectations changing, competitors taking different directions, and advanced technologies causing the business landscape to change, leaders need to create a better future vision for the team, develop strategic plans to get there, and communicate to members how to realign the plan and inspire them to move toward the future vision.

Lastly, to create a highly engaged and productive team, the leader needs to take the five actions – engage, envision, empower, enable members and enhance systems, and environment. The leader needs to engage members to build trusting relationships. This will be the foundation for building teamwork. To help inspire and align members, the leader needs to envision the desired future state of the team. Then the leader must empower members to co-create action plans to achieve the team mission and vision. The leader should also enable members so that they can enhance their professional and personal competencies to perform their roles better. To increase operational effectiveness and efficiency, the leader needs to enhance work processes, systems, and environments. All of those five types of actions will work together to build a strong team culture.

We will discuss each of those leaders' actions in the next Chapter. I believe you will develop your specific action plans and ideas as you go through each Chapter.

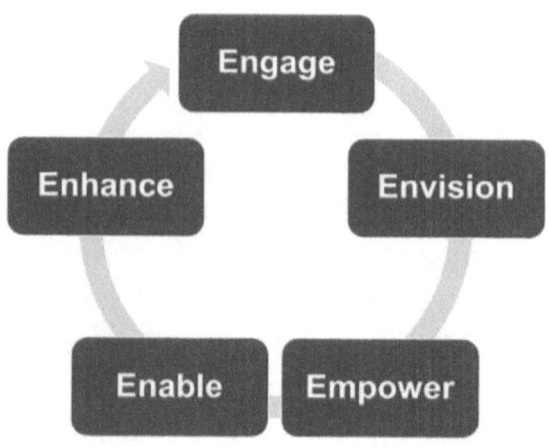

Chapter 4

Leadership Action 1 – Envision

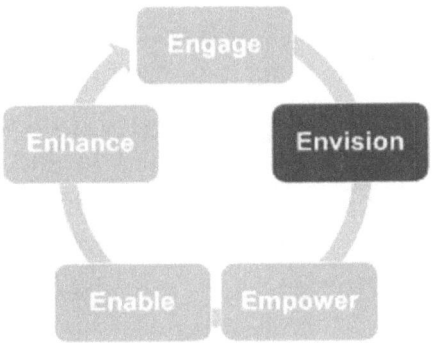

"Envisioning" Leadership

You have probably heard the story of bricklayers. While there are a several versions, the gist of the story goes like this. A traveler was walking along a path in a countryside and saw a bricklayer. He asked the bricklayer what he was doing. The bricklayer answered, "I am just laying those bricks day in and day out. I am so tired of this work." The traveler kept walking, found another bricklayer, and asked the same question. The second bricklayer responded, "I am laying bricks to build a cathedral, and I am working hard to finish my work as planned." The traveler kept walking, saw another bricklayer, and, again, asked the same question. The third bricklayer responded, "I am building a cathedral for people in this village, so that they can come, pray, and feel more fulfilled every day."

The first bricklayer in this episode didn't see the big picture of what he was doing. So, he is not much motivated in doing his work other than to get paid for what he is doing. The second bricklayer certainly understands the outcome from his work, but he might not have thought about what that can do for people in the village. The third bricklayer certainly saw the meaning in his work beyond its physical output, that is, making the village's people feel more fulfilled and happier. So, he was very engaged in his work and really committed to achieving his larger purpose and mission.

Are your members all like the third bricklayer, or are some of them like the first or second bricklayer?

Mediocre team leaders communicate tasks to the team so that they know what to do at least. Good team leaders set clear goals so that the team knows exactly what to do with a clear expectation of its final outcome. Great team leaders establish an inspiring and meaningful purpose and specific outcome so that all the members are motivated and committed to achieving the team results, including the contribution to customers and stakeholders.

What: "Envisioning" is to create an inspiring common purpose and goals for all members to understand and strive for. It's a must-do leadership action, which goes beyond setting a numerical goals and key performance measures, to building a committed, productive, and aligned team.

Why: As a series of research indicates, people are looking for meaning in their work, and meaningful work is one of key motivating factors for members to stay and thrive in their organization (https://www.fastcompany.com/3032126/how-to-find-meaning-during-your-pursuit-of-happinessat-work). The purpose of envisioning is to inspire and align the team around the common goal - team mission, vision, values, and strategic focus. It helps the members identify a meaning in their work, values, and key priorities.

Having a common team mission and vision will help the team understand specifically what they need to achieve and why they need to achieve it for their customers. As all the members see the what and why of the entire team, the common purpose and vision will unite the team to work together toward achieving it. So, it lays the foundation for teamwork and collaborative spirit in the team.

Key Leadership Action Areas: Key leadership actions for envisioning are:

1) **Create the mission and/or vision of the team.** A Mission is a reason for being or why we exist. I use a mission and a purpose interchangeably as both indicates the reason for being. The team mission indicates its target stakeholders and the values it adds to them. The vision is the future state of the team and an ideal world the team is creating - it gives clarity to what the team is striving to achieve in

the future. The team mission and vision need be meaningful, inspiring, vivid, and clear, so that team members can clearly visualize and feel motivated and inspired to continuously work for the team to achieve it.

Some teams have both a mission and a vision. Other teams have only one of them. Some other teams have integrated them into one. There is no strict rule in creating an inspiring direction for the team. Whatever works for your team is good.

2) **Create team values.** Team values are important guidelines for everyone in the team to follow. Team values will help the team work in a productive and collaborative manner. They will indicate the priority and also navigate the team to make the right choice in difficult situations. If your organization already has a set of company values, you may simply review, reiterate, and use it. We don't need to reinvent something that's already available.

Also, if there are priorities in the team values, it's wise to clarify them, so that your members can make the right judgment and take the right action when there are conflicts between values. For example, imagine you are running a manufacturing team, and your team values are efficiency, quality, speed, safety, teamwork, continuous improvement, and innovation, what will be your top, second and third priorities among those seven values? Quality and safety are usually ranked higher than innovation and efficiency, considering the customer needs for quality and members' need for safety.

3) **Develop the team's strategic focus.** The team strategy or key strategic focus provides an overarching core team theme or focal areas in the mid- to long-term. This will help the team stay on the right course over the long run with the right focus in mind, especially when under pressure and facing challenging situations. This will also guide members to coordinate and collaborate to achieve the team mission and vision.

See the below chart indicating typical characteristics of the team with and without "Envisioning." You may want to check the characteristics of your team members against the list below to understand the current level of "envisioning" in the team.

Characteristics of the team with and without "Envisioning"

Team Characteristics "with Envisioning"	Team Characteristics "without Envisioning"
• Clear about the big picture	• Don't see the big picture
• Motivated and committed to the work	• Not engaged in the work
• Results-focused, strong ownership	• Task-oriented mindset
• Mission and value-driven behaviors	• Task and rule-driven behaviors
• Energetic and proactive	• Lack of energy and reactive
• Focused on customers/stakeholders	• Focused on own or internal work
• Working to high-quality standards	• Work standards are not so high
• Working collaboratively in the team	• Not working well with others
• Resilient when under pressure	• Fragile and chaotic in bad times

Characteristics of Good Mission and Vision

1) **Inspiring** – The team mission and vision need to be inspirational in a way that members can identify a meaning and purpose of their work. So, it looks at the greater good, going beyond what each member can deliver individually. This will help the team to do their best to achieve great results. It also makes each member feel that they must grow themselves to perform to their full potential.

   Good: "We offer the best quality of ..."

   Poor: "We enjoy the best sales..."

2) **Externally focused** – A good mission and vision primarily focus on the customers and stakeholders the team is serving. So, it's not about selling more products or maximizing performance. External focus will help the entire team to work toward and collaborate to deliver the values their customers want. Good mission and vision are built upon understanding the customer's needs and wants as well as the market environment.

Good: "We offer the best customer experience in…"

Poor: "We are the number one…"

3) **Simple** - Good mission and vision statements are often simple and crisp so that people can easily remember them. If they are too long and complex, we cannot quickly grasp what the team is about or what it is creating for its stakeholders, customers, or external world. It shouldn't be like a shopping list of what the team does. Less is more.

4) **Unique** – A good mission and vision are unique, and they differentiate the team from other similar teams. When crafted well, both members and stakeholders can easily recognize and identify them with the team, as they carry the smell and color or unique intention and capability of the team that other teams do not have or claim.

Case Example

A product team of a pharmaceutical company was newly established, and they were tasked to develop several lines of optical medicines. There are 30 members in the team. One of the challenges they had was the team members had Various experience. It implies that the experiences were different - some are from non-pharmaceutical industries, and some others are newly joined from competitive companies. Half of the members knew each other, coming from different lines of business in the same company, and the rest of the members do not know anyone in the team. The newly formed team members do not appear to be comfortable or confident about working well each other in this circumstance. And, the leader of the team has relatively short experience in the company, joining a year ago. What would you do if you were in his shoes?

The leader saw this situation a bit challenging, and he wanted to create a positive start for this team. He hired an external consultant to facilitate a team kick-off meeting and several follow-up sessions to glue this less coherent team with a variety of backgrounds and experiences. Working with the consultant, the leader determined the overall steps and flow of the team meetings, and he set a specific agenda for the kick-off meeting.

During the initial team meeting, after spending some time to get to know each other so that they can share their ideas and thoughts comfortably and without much fear of conflicts when discussing those topics in a rather large group, the optical medicine team worked together to create its team mission and values.

This optical medicine team's mission statement goes "We help those who want to see the world." All members in that team were very inspired and excited about this team mission. The mission also united the members' minds and helped the team feel committed to working together to achieve the mission. The team mission became the glue of this originally a bit fragmented team.

Inspiring team mission is one of the keys to the team success. Furthermore, the process of creating the team mission and values and how the members are involved are critical in "Envisioning." So, let's see what actions team leaders should take to make a successful envisioning.

How: There are several ways for a team to create its mission and vision. One way is a top-down approach where the team leader creates and informs the team. Another way is asking team members to create. The third way is to co-create among the team leader and members.

In the spirit of self-directed and autonomous teams, I suggest we use co-creation approach, involving all the team members in this important planning process. The leader's role is to set the tone and orchestrate the envisioning activities.

> "Human beings commit to what they say."

Key Leadership Actions to Envision

1. Create the Team Mission

Goal: All members are clear about what they will achieve for their stakeholders and customers in the long run.

Action: Hold a team meeting or workshop to create the team mission. This can be done in one team meeting (2 - 4 hours, depending on how clear the team members are about why the team exists and also the number of roles in the team).

Preparation/Materials Needed: Flip charts, many stacks of PostIt notes (2.5 x 2.5 inches), and markers in many colors.

Example Flow:

1) Announce the session objective, e.g., We talked about the overall purpose and role of our team. But I am not very sure if all of us have the same thing in mind about our team mission. So, I want all of us to work together to create our team mission...

2) Describe an expected outcome on a whiteboard or flip-chart. The top of the flip-chart shows the headline - our mission statement. Under the headline, there are several bullet points of our specific achievements for our stakeholders.

3) Instruct the session flow (see below activities) and time frame.

4) Important stakeholders or customers: Ask the participants to name important stakeholders or customers. Ask them to prioritize those stakeholders. Write the stakeholders in the order of priority.

5) Important deliverables: Ask the participants to brainstorm the team's important deliverables and contributions to those stakeholders, using PostIt notes (one idea on one PostIt note) Ask them to prioritize those deliverables and contributions.

Write the deliverables and contributions in the order of priority.

6) Ask the team to bring and place their determined team contributions and deliverables on PostIt notes beside the stakeholder group on the whiteboard or flipchart.

7) Review the stakeholders and our contributions to them, discuss and agree among the team.

8) Ask them to come up with mission statement, having those stakeholders and our contributions in mind.

9) Discuss and finalize the team mission statement as a team.

10) Ask how each team member feels about the mission and gain commitment.

11) Take a photo of the cover story and put it on the team website or intranet.

2. Create a "Cover Story" Vision

This is a fun and exciting activity to share ideas and visually create the desired

"A picture is worth a thousand words."

team future. Why do we use visuals for our mission and vision? In contrast to a rather plain, written vision statement, visuals are easily memorable.

Goal: All members are clear about what the team is delivering to their external and internal stakeholders. The whole team is fully excited and committed to making that happen individually and collaboratively.

Action: Run a team meeting or workshop to discuss and agree on important team values; 1 - 2 hour(s).

Preparation/Materials Needed: Flip charts or large cardboards, and several sets of colored markers both thick- and thin-pointed ones.

Example Flow:

1) Announce the session objective, e.g., Now we all understand why we are here together for we discussed our important stakeholders we are serving and what values we are providing them. However, we may not have the same picture of our future. The clearer we are about our future state, the faster we can achieve our

team mission. Having said that, I want all of us to work together to visually create our ideal future team vision, using a typical magazine's "Cover Story" format. We create OUR team's cover story on a flip-chart (or a cardboard). So, let's begin. Imagine we are in 20XX, 5 years has passed since our team kick-off. As we have made a significantly positive impact to our stakeholders, "XXX," the famous magazine, has featured our team's success…

2) Describe an expected outcome on a whiteboard or flip-chart. There are several formats for a cover story vision. In a simple version, the top of the flip-chart shows the headline - like our major achievement(s). Under the headline, there is an exciting visual that signifies our success or added-values. Under the visuals there are several bullet points of our specific achievements externally and internally.

3) Instruct the session flow (see below activities) and time frame.

4) Individual brainstorming: Ask each member to self-brainstorm and write ideal

team results and contributions on PostIt notes - one ideal behavior on one PostIt note.

5) Stop and ask the team to bring all the PostIt notes to the front or around a whiteboard or flip-chart.

6) Ask the team to share and place the Post-It notes on the wall or whiteboard.

7) Group the shared desired team achievements written on PostIt notes.

8) Select most exciting and meaningful achievements (no more than 10) by voting.

9) Finalize the headline that best describes the team's contributions in the most exciting manner, and complete the team "Cover Story," including the exciting visuals.

10) Ask how each team member feels about the cover story and gain commitment.

11) Take a photo of the cover story and put it on the team website or intranet.

3. Create team "Vision Board"

This is another fun and exciting activity to share ideas and visually create the desired state of future team.

Goal: All members are clear about what the team is all about - who we are, what we deliver, and what we value, and all the members are energized and committed to making this happen individually and collaboratively. (Please see an example on the next page.)

Action: Run a team meeting or workshop to discuss and agree on important team values; 1 - 3 hour(s) depending on the team size.

Preparation/Materials Needed: Flip-chart or large cardboard, lots of magazines, scissors, glue, and several sets of colored markers and pens.

Example Flow:

1) Announce the session objective.

2) Describe an expected outcome. Lots of visuals and photos cut from any magazines and words that best describe our

team - who we are, what we deliver, how we work together, or what we value, placed or written on a cardboard or flipchart. There are no strict rules in creating a vision board.

3) Instruct the session flow (see below activities) and time frame.

4) Individual brainstorming: Remind the team of the mission or intent of the team. Ask each member to self-brainstorm and visualize the ideal of the team, flip through lots of magazines and cut out photos that best match your ideal team state, contributions or even bi-products on the way. Also, tell the members to write key words or phrases that signify the team successes on Post-It notes. Get the team excited, imaginative, and feeling their ideal...

5) Stop and ask the team to bring all the photos to the center.

6) Ask the team to share, indicate the intent, and put the photos on the floor.

7) Group those photos and select the most exciting and meaningful ones.

8) Ask the team to share and decide key words that go with the selected photos.

9) Ask the team to coordinate selected photos and words on a flip-chart or cardboard.

10) Ask how each team member feels about the vision board and gain commitment.

11) Take a photo of the vision board and put it on the team website or intranet.

THE SECRET OF HIGH IMPACT LEADERS

4. Create Team Values

Team values are a set of values we expect all members to value and abide by when working in the team - values that are important for the team to effectively deliver the team mission and vision. A good set of team values will help the team guide and align on what to focus on, how to work together in the team, and how to prioritize.

Goal: All members are clear about what the team values are, along with the priority of those values if appropriate.

Action: Run a session to discuss and agree on important team values in the team; 1 - 2 hour(s) depending on the team size.

Preparation/Materials Needed: Flip-chart, a several stacks of PostIt notes (2.5 x 2.5 inches), and markers.

Example Flow:

1) Announce the session objective.

2) Instruct the session flow (see below activities) and time frame.

3) Individual brainstorming: Review and remind the team of their mission and vision. Ask each member to self-brainstorm and write important values necessary for the team to follow to productively and collaboratively achieve the team mission and vision on PostIt notes - one value on one PostIt note. (10 minutes).

4) Stop and ask the team to bring all the Post-It notes to the front or around a whiteboard or wall (to put Post-It notes).

5) Ask the team to share and place the Post-It notes on the wall or whiteboard.

6) Group the team values shared on Post-It notes. Have those similar combined or integrated into one.

7) Select and prioritize important values. Keep them to 10.

8) Review, wordsmith, and finalize the team values.

9) Ask how each team member practice the principles and gain commitment.

10) Put the final team values on the team website or intranet.

5. Create strategic team focus

The team strategy or strategic team focus will align and navigate the team over the course of attaining the team mission and vision long-term. It will help the team coordinate and collaborate, focusing on the right priorities to achieve common objectives, beyond individuals' roles and responsibilities.

Goal: All members are clear about what the team's key milestones and/or focuses are, and also the priority of those focuses. Please see an example format on the next page.

Action: Run a strategic planning meeting to discuss and agree on important team priorities; 2 - 4 hour(s) depending on the team members' understandings of the team mission, stakeholders, and environment.

Preparation/Materials Needed: Flip-chart or wall-paper (with the team mission and vision), a several stacks of PostIt notes (2.5 x 2.5 inches), and markers.

Please note that if the team is working on a totally new project, the leader needs to ask the members to study the market, customers, stakeholders, competitors, and macro environment so that all members can participate in the session without feeling lost.

Example Flow:

1) Announce the session objective. (See the above description.)

2) Describe an expected outcome.

   Example outcome - team mission and key achievements (To-be) listed in the right-hand column, team's current status (As-is) shown on the left-hand side. Possible trends of key customers, market, competitors, and macro environment (Environmental trends) are listed at the bottom. Key important achievements and focuses (Key milestones) on the way to the team mission/vision are indicated in the middle of the sheet.

3) Instruct the session flow (see below activities) and time frame.

4) Review the desired future state of the team (To-be) depicted from the team mission and vision listed in the right-hand column of the flip-chart. Check and confirm if everyone is clear on the team future.

5) Have the team discuss and agree on where the team is now (As-is). Have them report back their agreed "As-is" state of the team and write their response on the sheet. (10 - 20 minutes.)

6) Have the team share, discuss, and agree on possible trends of customers, stakeholders, market, competitors, and macro environment (Environmental trends). Have them report back their agreed "Environmental trends," and write their response on the sheet. (20 - 30 minutes.)

7) Ask the team to individually brainstorm key milestones the team must achieve between As-is and To-be and write their thoughts on PostIt notes (one idea on one PostIt note). (10 - 15 minutes.)

8) Have the team share, discuss, and agree on the team's key milestones. Ask them

to place their agreed milestones in the center of the flip-chart. (10 - 15 minutes.)

9) Review and finalize the team's strategic focuses as a team.

10) Put the final sheet on the team website or intranet.

Strategic Planning Format

As-Is (Current Status)	Strategic Plans	To-Be (Desired Future)
Business: Team:		Business: Team:
Environmental Trends/Changes:		

In Summary

An inspiring team mission, vision, values, and clear team milestones will help the team fully engaged with the work they do as well as with the team itself. These will also help the entire team align in a common direction, unite the members hearts and minds, and help the team work proactively and collaboratively toward achieving it. Further, the success of envisioning lies in its process, where team members work together, building on each other's thoughts and ideas. The leader's important job is getting members excited and collaborative to set and agree on the team's ideal future state and contributions that are meaningful and inspiring. (Please see dos and don'ts of envisioning leadership in the below chart.)

Envisioning Elements

Dos and Don'ts of leaders in Envisioning

Dos	Don'ts
• Show your excitement about envisioning • Clarify objectives and expected outcomes • Involve members in envisioning activities • Energize the team to collaboratively deliver expected outcomes • Navigate and coach the team when necessary	• Be lukewarm and not show any excitement about envisioning • Just delegate everything to the team without clarifying the what and why • Decide everything by yourself or have your own plan/hidden agenda • Do not encourage collaboration among the team • Do not support when the team gets stuck, or just override with own ideas

Chapter 5

Leadership Action 2 - Engage

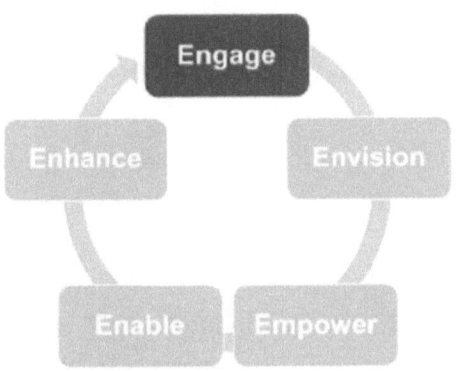

"Engaging" Leadership

Daniel Goleman (2000), the father of Emotional Quotient (EQ or Emotional Intelligence), conducted a very interesting study among managers to understand what leadership styles exist in the workplace, how each leadership style influences team performance, and when each different leadership style is effective.

His researchers identified six types of leadership styles:

1) Coercive - Top-down, telling type leadership style
2) Authoritative - Inspiring, visionary leadership style
3) Democratic - Participative leadership style
4) Affiliative - Harmony creating leadership style
5) Pacesetting - Forerunner type leadership style
6) Coaching - People developing leadership style

Which leadership style of the above is closest to yours? Which styles of leadership appear to be effective in delivering results? Which styles of leadership appear to be engaging?

Authoritative, democratic, affiliative, and coaching styles are more involving and engaging with the team. Coercive and pacesetting styles are more task-oriented with the least concern for people. How is that affecting their impact on the team's performance?

No style is perfect for all businesses and organization situations, and there exists the best-fit situation for each style. However, overall positive impact on the performance is highest for "Authoritative (visionary)" style, followed by "Democratic," "Affiliative," and then "Coaching" styles, as indicated by the research data. On the contrary, "Coercive" and "Pacesetting" style leaders create a negative impact on the team's performance in general.

The above research results suggest that (1) involving and engaging members can positively impact the team's performance, and (2) too much task focus with limited people involvement and care can negatively impact the team's performance.

What: "Engaging" is to build mutual understanding, trusting relationships, and a community in the team. The leader's job is to create opportunities for the team to mutually understand each other, build relationships, and communicate openly free of worry, all of which will make the team a highly engaging and collaborative community.

Why: One of the key ingredients of high-performance teams is "trust" among the team members. It takes time to build trust in the team. Further, as Harvard University's longitudinal study indicated, good relationships are a necessary ingredient for our health and long life. So, creating a connected, engaged, and trusted workplace is crucial for healthy and productive teams. The leader is in the best position to influence the members to build trust and a collaborative community in the team.

Leaders' attention, behaviors, and language will certainly create the culture of the team. Leaders need to role model the values and culture created in "envisioning" action. High-performance cultures nurture positivity, relationships, and trust in the team. Several studies indicate positive interactions and conversations are key to good performance. Workplace feedback survey experts, Nowack and Mashihi, suggest feedback is effective when the ratio of positive feedback to negative feedback is equal to or higher than 3:1. Heaphy and Losada studied leadership teams' interactions in the meeting, and found that the ratio of positive comments to negative comments of higher performance teams was 5.6:1 on average - positive talks consist of acknowledging, agreeing, supportive comments, and opinions; and negative talks are disagreeing, negating, unsupportive comments, and dialog. Relatedly, the longitudinal study by Gottman suggests that couples with positive-to-negative interaction ratio of 5:1 can enjoy a long-lasting marriage.

So, leaders have an important role in taking a lead in building and creating a positive, trusting, and collaborative culture in the team.

Key Leadership Action Areas: Key leadership actions for engaging are:

1) **Co-create team principles.** The objective of this action is to ensure all members are fully clear about expected behaviors and attitudes and to work together productively and collaboratively. It's like house rules that help all members in the house speak and behave in a respectful, positive, and cooperative way.

2) **Conduct a fun get-to-know-each-other meeting.** The objective of this action is to help all the members in the team understand one another at a deeper level, so they can feel closer and get connected

with each other on a personal level. Mutual understanding will help the team co-create a psychologically safer and happier workplace.

3) **Role model engagement, care, and trust to create a community.** Human beings learn from modeling or imitating behaviors of a role model. The objective of this action is for the leader to exhibit the desired team behaviors and mindset to influence the members to follow the leader's habits and behaviors to build an engaged, caring, and trusting culture in the team.

4) **Help members be self-aware of their communication habits and modify it as appropriate.** As we are not observing our own communication, we usually don't fully understand its strengths and weaknesses. This is about helping members increase their self-awareness of their communication habits, so that they can modify their current habits when needed.

5) **Help the team improve their communication style.** We all have different communication styles and preferences. Each

communication style can be effective in some situations but maybe not in others. The objective of this action is to deepen members' understanding of their communication styles and learn how to adjust them to best suit the styles of counterparts to facilitate effective communication in the team.

See the below chart indicating typical characteristics of the team with and without "Engaging."

Characteristics of the team with and without "Engaging."

Team Characteristics "with Engaging"	Team Characteristics "without Engaging"
• Understand each other • Communicates honestly and openly • Lots of positive talks • Actively listens to others • Asks for feedback • Gives honest feedback • Has healthy debates	• Don't know other members well • Doesn't tell true feelings and opinions • Many negative talks • Listens halfheartedly • Doesn't ask for feedback • Feedback is minimal • Avoids conflict and debate

• Asks for help • Proactively supports, coordinates and collaborates	• Tries to do by themselves • Poor supporting, coordination and collaboration in the team

Key Principles of Good Engaging

1) **Psychological safety** - All members feel safe and comfortable working with the team. They can always speak their minds, honest opinions, and feelings without worry.

2) **Full of respect and have supportive and trusting relationships** - All members feel they are fully respected, and members are supportive and cooperative. So they can always work confidently with growth and a resourceful mindset.

3) **Proactive communication and collaboration** - Members are passionate about working in the team to bring out the best in themselves, to unleash their full potential. This creates proactive communication and collaboration in delivering continuous improvements and innovation.

4) **Exemplary leadership** - The leader is the role model of ideal team behaviors, exhibiting the ideal and desired communication, trust, and communal behaviors.

Case Example

The HR team of company Z had long been divided by business unit and located in different cities. Two years ago, these separate HR groups were integrated into one team, as part of company Z streamlining initiative. This integration was not executed effectively, and thus, last year, a new HR leader was brought in from outside the company to replace the predecessor in implementing the project. The new HR leader has rolled up his sleeves to tackle this project, executed the planned integration, and now, all members car located in one office. However, a recent employee opinion survey run earlier this year revealed dysfunction and personnel issues in the HR team. The HR team's survey results indicated key improvement areas are trust, communication, collaboration, productive work environment, and goal clarity. Further investigation also surfaced that the customers of the HR team are not happy about their services.

Imagine you are brought into this team to replace the HR team leader and turn around this chaotic situation. What would you do to improve the HR team and their performance? Please recall the framework of high-performance teams. Which elements were missing in this HR team - clear direction, leadership effectiveness, role clarity, work system, communication and trusting relationship? Most of those factors appear to be broken, don't they? Then, what would be your primary focus for change?

What happened in this case was placing a tentative HR leader from another region to manage and correct the situation immediately, while searching for a new HR leader to join the company. I was called in as an external change facilitator to support the temporary HR leader in turning around the situation.

As the team was suffering from poor relationships and unclear goals while feeling lost, we initially focused on building the relationships while clarifying the team's direction moving forward. The whole team spent two days understanding each other's concerns and hopes, building better relationships, discussing a brighter future together and identifying key improvement areas moving forward. At the end of this kick-off meeting, some of the members who joined in the last year were so excited and said, "These two days were awesome, and I now know all my colleagues, and I feel close to them."

Later in the year, we had a few more team meetings and workshops to review and improve the team processes and systems, which improved the team's services and performance, resulting in improved customer satisfaction. However, those process and system improvements would not have been successful if we hadn't built the relationship among the team in the initial phase.

Trusting relationships are the bedrock of high-performance teams.

Key Leadership Actions to "Engage to build trust and community"

1. Co-create Team Principles.

Team principles are a set of ideal behaviors we expect all members to abide by and practice in the team, so that the team work together productively and collaboratively. Team principles are action-oriented, using a verb in the sentence, not a noun - such as "We respect and trust our colleagues," or "We go the extra mile to create better customer experience than our competitors." Team principles will work as guiding principles for the team to make the best decisions and take effective actions to achieve the team mission and vision. Also, team principles focus on the positives rather than the negatives, building on positive psychology. (So, we exclude the line, "We don't ...)

Goal: All members are clear about what behaviors are expected in the team and are fully committed to those new behaviors. (Please see an example on the next page.)

Action: Run a session to discuss and agree on ideal behaviors in the team; 1 - 1.5 hour.

Preparation/Materials Needed: Team values developed before, a few stacks of PostIt notes (2.5 x 2.5 inches).

Example Flow:

1) Announce the session objective, e.g., "Please recall we have created our team values along with our mission and vision so that we can all work productively and collaboratively. Today, I want all of us to work together to create our team princi-

ples, that is, "ideal behaviors in the team" - how each one of us work in the team to make our team highly productive, collaborative, ..."

2) Instruct the session flow:

   1) Do brain-writing using PostIt notes individually
   2) Share and group ideal behaviors (PostIt notes) as a group
   3) Identify and finalize team principles (ideal behaviors in the team)
   4) Confirm

3) Individual brainstorming: Ask each member to self-brainstorm and write ideal work behaviors on PostIt notes - one ideal behavior on one PostIt note. (10 minutes).

4) Stop and ask the team to bring all the PostIt notes with ideal behaviors to the front or around a whiteboard or wall (to put PostIt notes on).

5) Ask the team to share and place the PostIt notes on the wall or whiteboard.

6) Group the shared ideal behaviors on PostIt notes.

7) Select important behaviors by voting - no more than 10.

8) Double-check that the selected principles are in line with the team values.

9) Finalize the team principles, or ideal behaviors in the team.

10) Ask how each team member practices the principles and gain their commitment.

11) Send the final team principles to the team.

12) Do periodical progress reviews on how team principles are practiced in the team.

The Most Trusted R&D

We will bring creative ideas to life!

- ✓ We work as a team with a shared purpose.
- ✓ We respect and trust each other.
- ✓ We value the creativity to make a difference.
- ✓ We speak honestly and listen with open mind.
- ✓ We learn from each other.
- ✓ We act as a professional to meet customer needs.

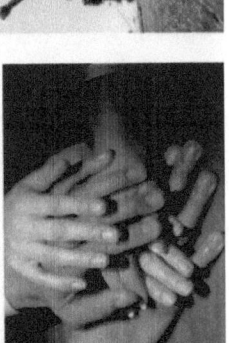
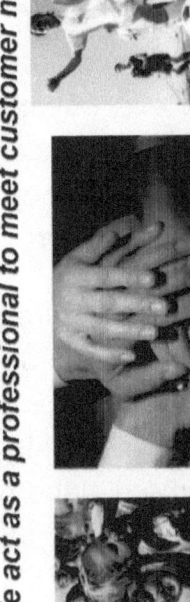
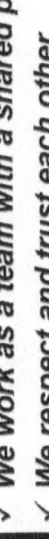

2. Conduct a Fun Get-to-know-each-other Meeting.

Goal: All members understand each other at a deeper level beyond their work life; into personal history, experiences and even personal values, and they feel they are heard and well understood by the team.

Action: There are a wide variety of activities for this mutual understanding session from a simple self-introduction informing where they are from, hobbies, recent fun events, next vacation plans, etc. to more elaborative ones, such as a pictorial life story.

"Pictorial life story" As many of you might have experienced simple self-introductions, I will introduce you a "pictorial life story." I have done this activity hundreds of times for various groups on many different occasions ranging from a new team start-up meeting to a multi-company project kick-off meeting, to an existing team's re-energizing meeting, and it worked great on all occasions. Participants really enjoyed the activity, and importantly, remembered their colleagues' stories more vividly, as a pictorial story or visuals are more memorable than other forms.

In this session, all participants, including the leader, will draw a picture on a sheet of paper that shows the high points from their personal history in four blocks - memorable experience or scene form (1) childhood, (2) student days, (3) work life, and (4) personal life/event. Each member will spend 3 - 5 minutes for their self-introduction; 1 - 2 hours depending on the number of participants. (Please see an example on the next page.)

Preparation/Materials Needed: a sheet of paper for all participants (preferably bigger than Letter or A4 size to be visible from a distance. If you have more than 20 people in the room), sets of colored markers (Mr. Sketch - thick and thin ones).

Flow:

1) Announce the meeting objective, e.g., As we all want to become an even happier and more collaborative team, I want each and every one of us to really get to know each other, like family...

2) Instruct the preparation activity, e.g., For that, I want you to prepare and introduce

yourself visually and vividly to the rest of the team. In preparation for your self-introduction, I want you to identify and draw the memorable experiences or events in your life - first, during your childhood, second, student days, third, work life, and lastly, your personal life... Please use colored markers, and make it colorful to represent your memorable experience or events...

3) Give 15 minutes to complete their drawing. After 15 minutes, ask the team to bring their drawings to the front table. You will shuffle the stack of drawings, keeping the stack backside up.

4) Pull out one drawing from the stack, ask whose drawing it is. After identifying its owner, ask her/him to come up front and do the self-introduction for 3 - 5 minutes. After completion, she/he will pull out one drawing from the stack, and ask for the owner to do their self-intro.

5) #4 will continue until everyone finishes the self-intro.

6) Ask the team to reflect and share their findings and thoughts from this exercise. This can be done in a small group if the group is more than 20.

7) Keep the pictorial self-introduction sheet in the team room or upload to the team intranet.

3. Demonstrate Engagement, Care, and Trust to Create a Community.

Leaders need to lead by example. So, the leader needs to proactively communicate with each and every one of team members with respect, trust, and active listening to understand their situations, thoughts, ideas, emotions, and concerns. Like kids learn from observing parents and older kids, members will learn from observing good communication and interpersonal skills role modeled by their leaders.

Goal - All members feel engaged and trusted by the leader, and then, become wanting to respect, care, trust, support, and collaborate with each other in the team.

Actions:

1) **Communicate your intent for your new or strengthened behaviors to build a community full of respect, care, and trust** - If you want to start new or strengthened communication with the team, it's usually wise to declare your intent and expectation before you start. Otherwise, your members might likely feel a bit uneasy or even skeptical when they

notice your changed communication, greetings, and behaviors without knowing why you do such things - just like your friends or partner feel strange when they notice you change your communication style and habits without telling them of your intention.

2) **Lead by example** - Increase self-awareness of the characteristics of your own communication behaviors, habits, and mindset, and improve them as necessary while continuing strong ones.

Example Activities:

(1) Ask yourself the following questions to understand your current trust level in the team and your possible new actions to each team member:

> How is each member of my team engaged with me?
> How is each member trusting and supporting other members in the team?
> How am I being trusted by each member?

How do I exhibit my respect to each member now?

How do I exhibit my care to each member now?

How do I exhibit my trust to each member now?

What new communication and behaviors should I exhibit to each member from today?

(2) Determine what specific behaviors you want to roll model to instill ideal behaviors in the team. Write those ideal leader's behaviors or habits in your journal or on a sheet of paper or computer screen with specific goals for each of your role model behavior and keep them visible to remind you from time to time.

(3) At the end of every day, reflect on your behaviors and actions of the day, and check how well you have practiced those role model behaviors with the team. Self-reflection and follow-up is key for the success of the role modeling practice or any behavioral change. Dr. Marshall Goldsmith, one of the most admired executive coaches, even articulates the importance

of daily self-reflection, indicating he himself does self-reflection every day with his assistant, as, otherwise, he may forget doing the reflection himself as he is very busy.

Hint:

a) Dr. Goldsmith suggests we should ask ourselves a positive and proactive question on a daily basis to enhance our ownership for strengthening habits and behaviors. For example, "I do my best to engage with my team today," "I do my best to build a community of trust in every moment today." Or, "Did I do my best to engage my team today?" or "Did I do my best to build a community of trust in every moment today" for using as a daily checking and reflection question.

b) Keeping a personal journal will also work very well to reflect and review progress of our daily behaviors. It doesn't have to be a long journal. It can be only a few sentences.

4. Help members become self-aware of their communication habits and modify them as appropriate using the "Johari" window model.

We all understand open communication and feedback is critical for high-performance teams, as they will help enhance timely communication, improve decision-making and problem-solving quality, resulting in faster improvements and innovation in the marketplace. This action will help the team understand how well each member is practicing open communication, using feedback from other members in the team.

Why do we need to get input or feedback on our behaviors or actions from others? Because we are not watching our behaviors from outside and don't really know how our behaviors look from other's perspectives. So, with others' feedback, we can learn and close the gap between our perception of our behaviors, and those of others, and then, improve our communication quality.

Goal: All members become aware of their open communication levels based on other's perception, and they can identify where they need to be more open in their communication and be fully committed to practicing more open communication.

Action: Run a session to discuss and agree on ideal behaviors in the team; 1 - 1.5 hour.

Preparation/Materials Needed: Flip-chart/Wallpaper (one for each member), a stack of PostIt notes (2.5 x 2.5 inches) for each member.

Example Flow:

1) Announce the goal and flow: e.g., "Today we will be increasing our self-awareness and identify our further strengthening areas in our communication to make our team further high performing. "

2) Introduce the "Johari Window", its concept, and how to use it. (See attached example.) The Johari Window is often used to increase self-awareness and identify improvement opportunities for communication and behaviors. There are two factors in the Johari Window. The first factor is what you know about yourself. The second factor relates to what other people know about you. The model works using four area quadrants. Anything you

know about yourself is part of your "Open" area. Next, any aspect that you do not know about yourself, but others within the group are aware of, is in your "Blind" area. There are also aspects about yourself that you are aware of but have not told others, this quadrant is your "Hidden" area. The last area is the "Unknown" area - unknown to you and anyone else.

Members in high-performance teams usually have wide "Open" areas because they practice open communication freely, sharing their thoughts, feelings, and feedback in the team. We can build trust in the team by disclosing information to others and learning about others from the information they, in turn, disclose about themselves. With the help of feedback from others, we can become aware of some of your positive and negative traits as perceived by others and overcome some of the personal issues that may be inhibiting your personal or group dynamics within the team. Now each of us will create our Johari Window to deepen our self-understanding as well as to identify our improvement opportunities.

3) Ask the team to write 10 strong points and 10 suggestions for improvement for themselves in terms of communication and team behaviors - writing one point on one PostIt note; 5 minutes.

4) Ask the team to make a "Johari Window" on a flip-chart for themselves, drawing a vertical line and horizontal line in the middle of the flip-chart. (One flip-chart per member.) Ask them to keep their PostIt notes with their self-perceptions on for a while until instructed.

5) Ask the team to write 3 strong points and three suggestions for improvement for other members, spending about 3 minutes for each member multiplied by the number of members. Please note you will hand out the feedback to the team, please write it in a way the receiver will be able to receive it easily; so, write it nicely, not harshly. (This usually needs about 2 minutes for writing feedback for one member.)

6) Stop the team when the allocated time is over and ask them to collect and hand out

their feedback to each member of the team.

7) Ask the team to fill up their "Johari Window" with the PostIt notes with others' feedback as well as their own perspectives (written at step 3). Their perspectives will be placed on either "Open" or "Hidden" windows. Others' feedback will be placed on "Open" or "Blindspot" windows.

8) Ask the team to review their Johari Window to identify improvement areas for their future communication or behaviors in the team and decide the top 3 action plans.

9) Ask the team to share their key findings, insights, and indicated actions moving forward. This can be done in a small group if the group size is too large.

You may want to ask the team to find buddies and do buddy-coaching in a trio once a month or so.

Johari Window

	Self-Perception	
	Known to Self	Not known to Self
Known to Others	Open	Blind Spot
Not known to Other	Hidden	Unknown

(Perceptions of others)

5. Help the Team Improve Communication Style.

Communication is crucially important when strengthening team culture as well as team performance. So, the better each member communicates with other team members, the more productive and collaborative the team can become.

Our communication style and habits are based on our values, beliefs, personality, and individual culture shaped since childhood. So, understanding our own beliefs, perspectives, preferences, and personality will help us understand why we communicate the way we do, which will help us improve and strengthen our communication.

Goal: All members become more aware of communication styles and habits of their own and of other members, and why so. Eventually, they will identify their communication strengths and improvement areas and become committed to strengthening their communication habits and styles to improve communication and collaboration in the team.

Action: Run a session to understand each members' communication styles, habits, strengths, and improvement areas, using a psychometric assessment tool, such as DiSC, MBTI, or Big 5 model; share the communication styles and characteristics; and agree on how each member can modify their communication in the team to achieve better team communication and performance; 3 hours to a half day.

For your information, DiSC indicates there are 4 behavioral characteristics in each of us ahd had we behave differently depending on the levels of those 4 characteristics. MBTI, Myers Briggs Type Indicator suggests there are 16 types of personality, depending on the four dimensions — where we focus our attention and get energy (extraversion versus introversion), how we take in information and the kind of information we like (sensing versus intuition), how we make decisions (thinking versus feeling, and how we orient ourselves to our life or the external world (judging versus perceiving). (Please see the framework of DiSC and MBTI on the next page.)

Preparation/Materials Needed:

1) If you are not certified in any psychometric assessment tool, contact a certified practitioner to facilitate the session.

2) Have all members complete one psychometric assessment one week prior to the session. Have all assessment reports printed.

Example Flow:

1) Announce the session goal, flow, and expected outcome from the session.

2) Ask members to identify and share challenging or difficult communication situations in pairs with other team members. Tell them to identify how to solve that

challenge and improve team communication by the end of the session.

3) Brief the assessment tool overview, objective, key assessment dimensions, characteristics of each communication type or style (to be done by a certified practitioner of the tool).

4) Do a series of group activities to better understand the characteristics, strengths, and watch-outs of each style or type.

5) Have the team members review their report to understand the characteristics, strengths, and risks of their communication style or type better.

6) Ask them to share their style or type, and how they want to modify their communication within the team.

7) Communicate how the team will follow-up on their action plans.

You may want to ask the team to find buddies and do buddy-coaching in trios once a month or so.

THE SECRET OF HIGH IMPACT LEADERS

DISC Behavioral Profiler

Fast-paced/Outspoken

Conscientiousness	Dominance
• Analytical	• Direct
• Reserved	• Driving
• Precise	• Competitive
• Private	• Determined
• Accurate	• Forceful
• Meticulous	• Results-oriented
Steadiness	**Influence**
• Adaptable	• Outgoing
• Systematic	• Optimistic
• Patient	• Inspiring
• Humble	• Persuasive
• Relaxed	• Lively
• Even-tempered	• High-spirited

Accepting/Warm — Questioning/Skeptical

Cautious/Reflective

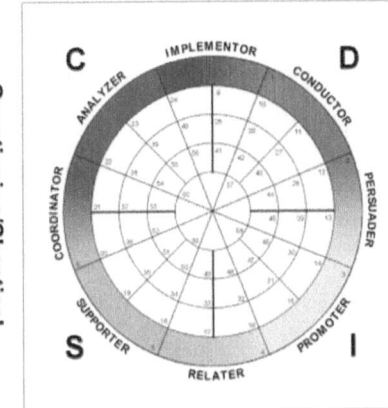

Myers Briggs Type Indicator

- Extraversion: **E** or **I** : Introversion
- Sensing: **S** or **N** : Intuition
- Thinking: **T** or **F** : Feeling
- Judging: **J** or **P** : Perceiving

16 Personality Types

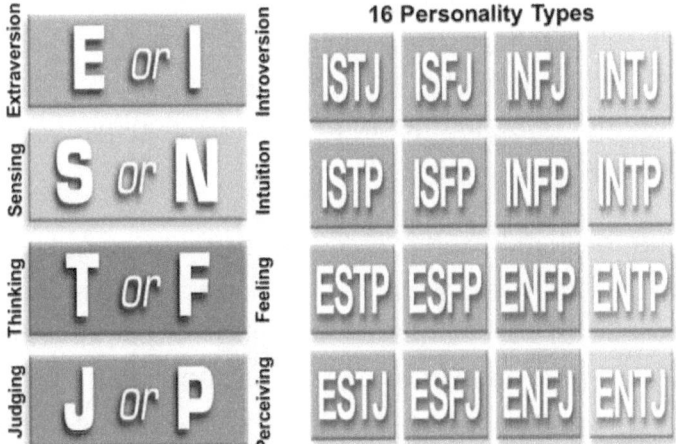

ISTJ, ISFJ, INFJ, INTJ
ISTP, ISFP, INFP, INTP
ESTP, ESFP, ENFP, ENTP
ESTJ, ESFJ, ENFJ, ENTJ

In Summary

Top-down goal-setting and planning is a sure way to discourage and demotivate the team. Autonomy and self-directedness will be key drivers for engaging and motivating the team to do their best to achieve the team mission and vision. The leader will promote true empowerment through putting members in the driver's seat, so that they take ownership to analyze, plan, implement, reflect, and achieve their mission. Also, those will help the entire team align in the common direction, unite the members hearts and minds, and help the team work proactively and collaboratively toward achieving it. The ultimate goal of "empowering" is to energize the whole team to become excited about bringing out the best in the members to achieve their peak performance.

The leader's important job is to truly delegate to the team this important work individually and collaboratively while respecting, trusting, and supporting each member throughout this whole empowering process. (Please see dos and don'ts of engaging leadership in the below chart.)

Dos and Don'ts of leaders in Engaging

Dos	Don'ts
• Respect and trust each and everyone in the team • Truly delegate • Stay energetic, excited, and positive • Show high expectation • Be accessible • Energize the team to deliver expected outcomes • Create alignment, co-learning, and celebration opportunities • Give feedback and coaching whenever possible and appropriate	• Be skeptical about members capability • Delegate partially • Stay lukewarm or pessimistic • Fail to express your expectation • Be laissez-faire • Be unexcited about members efforts and achievements • Fail to connect with the team to align, learn together, and celebrate • Fail to support when members need feedback and support

Chapter 6

Leadership Action 3 - Empower

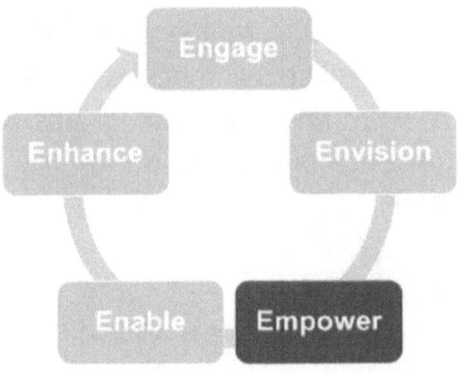

"Empowering" Leadership

How do you determine the annual work plans of your team? Who sets the goals? Who makes the plans - the leader or member? How do you review the progress of the team's results and performance?

Productivity at manufacturing companies significantly improved in early 1900s, as manufacturers started adopting the concept of "scientific management" by Frederick Taylor into their operations. Taylor, the father of scientific management, made many contributions to creating a productive workplace through a series of studies and experiments, such as his time and motion studies to identify how the task needs to be performed to achieve optimal productivity by careful selection of workers who fit the job, a division of labor, and making the task as small as possible to minimize mistakes (also needed when there were still many immigrants who were not fluent in English coming in the United States in early 1900s).

While Taylor had a balanced view of running a productive workplace with both scientific production management and healthy, collaborative human (or manager-worker) relationships, many organizations mostly adopted his scientific production management with little or no concern of collaborative human systems that result in dehumanized workplaces. Dehumanized — an overly productivity-focused workplace was depicted in Charles Chaplin's "Modern Times." In the movie, each worker is working on a single task - tightening bolts, hitting plates, and so on and so forth, without talking or coordinating the work with their neighbor, all under supervisors who kept checking on and shouting at the workers.

As illustrated in Chaplin's "Modern Times," in the earlier management cycle of "plan-do-check-adjust," managers did all of the "planning," members did all of "doing," managers did "checking" and members did all "adjusting" work. So in the past, managers were expected to do all the thinking, and members were enforced to do all the activities. What impact could this type of work setting create in the workplace? Of course, it certainly lowered employees' motivation and morale.

Hence, there was a shift in academic and management researchers' minds from too much emphasis on productivity to a humanitarian approach to address human needs for connectedness and safety in the workplace. Beyond meeting fundamental human needs, what should we, as leaders, should do to further engage members with their work? It's autonomy and self-directedness that engage and motivate members in their work. People are more committed to what they say they do. This is especially true when they thought through, carefully planned, and determined their actions.

How is self-directedness and autonomy implemented in our current workplace? Gallup research indicates 7 out of 10 employees are not satisfied with how their goal is being set as they are not involved in setting them (https://www.gallup.com/workplace/231620/why-performance-development-wins-workplace.aspx). This indicates that we have not made much progress from the work coordination of the early 1900s - most thinking and planning is done by managers! How much autonomy and self-directedness do your members have in performing their roles?

> "Build an autonomous and self-directed culture"

What: "Empowering" is to give members the power to explore and execute their plans to achieve the goals. So, leaders should encourage members to "plan-do-check-adjust" work until completing their roles, without insisting their top-down goals. For this to happen, members must study their customers and market situations, explore opportunities, set goals and plans, implement those plans, review the progress, and consolidate or modify the plans to best achieve the goals. To support members, the leader's roles are empowering members, and providing support as appropriate or necessary.

Why: Autonomous and self-directed work systems will generate and enhance members' ownership, as indicated in many experiments and research, such as the Tavistock studies. Autonomy or self-directedness are the key motivators for human beings to keep tackling the task until its completion. Also, people are more committed to what they say they do, rather than what they were told to do by someone else.

An autonomous and self-directed way of working are key to creating a highly engaged and productive workplace. In this VUCA (volatile, uncertain, complex, and ambiguous) economy, leaders do not have all the answers and cannot direct members timely and correctly. So, members need to be fully empowered to get the job done timely and with strong ownership.

What are you currently doing when setting and aligning goals for members? How clear do you think each of your members are about their annual goals and plans? If you think that's clear, how did you confirm the goals are crystal clear to each of your members?

For your information, one of the key reasons why a performance management system is not working for some organizations is the goal-setting and planning process where the manager semi-dictates the goal of members without their true commitment. Many frustrations occur when expectations are not aligned and not met in the end, such as customer's frustration when their expectation was not understood and not delivered by service or product providers. Likewise, few members are clear about their specific goals aligned with their manager. When this happens, performance appraisal meetings will be miserable. Therefore, expectation matching, or aligning specific goals between the manager and the member is critical.

How to align the goal is important. The bad way for setting goals is for boss to direct or dictate the goal and numbers, regardless of what members think and feel about those goals. This top-down goal-setting approach will also be a sure way to make the performance review meetings a failure as members did not buy-in and agree to their goals in the first place. So, if your members are not happy about their performance review meetings, goal-setting may be an area for improvement. It's not the goal itself, but how the goal is set and agreed that makes a difference in member's commitment, motivation, growth, and performance.

Key Leadership Action Areas: Key leadership actions around empowering are:

1) **Empower members to develop their long-term achievements.** Building on a team's strategic milestones identified during "envisioning" session, the leader will involve the team members in identifying the key mid- to long-term achievements to actualize the team mission and vision. The leader energizes and facilitates the team discussion.

2) **Empower members to individually develop annual goals and work plans.** The leader empowers members to analyze market and customer needs and competitors and environments, think

through and set annual goals for their roles, and develop annual work plans to achieve their goals. The leader gives feedback or coaching as necessary.

3) **Empower members to coordinate and align annual team plans.** The leader empowers members to align and coordinate their annual plans to optimize the team performance. The leader supports team collaboration by facilitating the meeting, giving feedback, or coaching as needed.

4) **Energize members to implement and achieve their work plans.** The leader empowers and energizes members to fully implement and complete their work plans. The leader acknowledges their actions, praises their wins, gives feedback, and coaches.

5) **Celebrate members' achievements.** The leader creates the opportunity for the team members to share key achievements and learning, and to celebrate wins and the team progress together as a team.

See the below chart indicating typical characteristics of a team with and without "Empowering." You may want to check characteristics of your team members against the list below to understand the current level of empowering in the team.

Characteristics of the team with and without "Empowering"

Team Characteristics "with Empowering"	Team Characteristics "without Empowering"
• Clear about the what and why of their annual goals and plans	• Not sure about the what and why of their annual goals and plans
• Exhibits strong ownership	• Exhibits passive attitudes at work
• Focuses on meeting customer needs	• Focuses on their own needs and to-do lists
• Constantly looks for improvements	• Does what's on the plan and doesn't go extra miles
• Explores opportunities for innovation	
• Respects and trusts team members	• Stays away from trying new things
• Communicates and	• Does not fully re-

collaborates smoothly in the team • Moves fast and takes action timely	spect and trust other members • Minimal communication and collaboration in the team • Cautious about making moves

Key Principles of Good Empowering

1) **Member-centered** – Often, the leader takes the lead when developing annual team goals and plans, but he/she should not dictate the specific annual goals and plans. Instead, members are fully charged in developing their own goals and action plans. This is an effective way to generate true ownership and accountability in members, leading to increased motivation and engagement.

2) **Collaboration in the team** - The leader needs to encourage the team to collaborate and create synergy to maximize team performance. The team collaborates best when there is trust in the team, as trust is the foundation of teamwork and collaboration. So, the leader needs to help build

trust in the team and also personally exhibit and role model trusting behaviors, so members will follow.

3) **Data-based decision-making** - While the leader empowers the member to take ownership in analyzing, developing annual plans, implementing, evaluating, and completing the plans, he or she needs to ensure all the members are making the right judgments and decisions, based on appropriate data and information. This is important in making optimal decisions and keeping the team from unnecessary risks. There should be no blind trust.

4) **Supportive leadership** - The leader needs to fully empower the member so that they feel energized about planning, implementing, and completing their roles. Nevertheless, the leader needs to offer support to the member when appropriate. Full empowerment and delegation is not a laissez-faire leadership, which is a total hands-off, letting members set rules and determine plans and rules without any intervention from the leader.

Case Example

Product marketing teams of a consumer goods company are fully empowered and delegated to maximize branding and market share. Each product team is self-directed and has virtually full autonomy to build their business as long, as their actions are in line with the corporate values and following its marketing principles and business planning cycle. They all have growth mentality and healthy dissatisfaction toward the current status, so they always shoot for double-digit growth even in a stagnant market.

Each product team does their best in analyzing market situations, customers' unmet needs, identifying new user insights, strengthening or modifying product strategies, and creating and implementing better marketing initiatives continuously year after year.

Each member of the product team has a role to play - some are working on consumer promotion, others are working on trade promotion, some others are responsible for online and digital marketing. The product team manager empowers each member and brings the best out in members to fully utilize their power and potential. Under the empowering leadership, members individually do a thorough analysis of their stakeholders and benchmarking competitors to be on top of what they do. Regardless of their age, tenure, and gender, their proposed ideas are accepted as long as they show the evidence of winning possibilities and business viability.

The product teams reflect on executed marketing and promotion plans periodically, so that the team can identify success factors by determining improvement areas for the next year. They also share their learning with other product teams to maximize their learning and future success probability. All the product teams enjoy either top market share or second share in their respective product category.

Apparently, empowering leadership that allows self-directedness and autonomy of each member is a driving force for the product marketing team to identify and implement an innovative marketing campaign and win in the marketplace year after year.

Key Leadership Actions to "Empower"

1. Empower members to develop their long-term achievements.

Most teams immediately work on annual goals and plans with or without a team mission and vision. This can create a short-term focused, narrow mindset in the team without much thinking about their long-term vision or contributions to the stakeholders. Or some members may only think about their own role without linking it to the larger team mission.

Thinking of a long-term goal will help us think big and build growth mindset. By having all members develop their mid-term achievements and share them in the entire team, you can build a more long-term mindset and collaborative emotion in the team. Also, this collaborative session will be especially effective when the team has several different roles, as each member gets feedback from the rest of the team, so they can modify their ideas during the session.

Goal: All members are clear about and committed to what the team will deliver in 2 - 5 years to collaboratively achieve team mission.

Action: This can be done in one team meeting (2 to 4 hours, depending on the number of members and the roles in the team), or divided into a few separate meetings including some pre-assignment work.

Preparation/Materials Needed: The developed team mission and vision, flip charts (a few sheets of paper for each role), and many stacks of PostIt notes (2.5 x 2.5 inches).

Example Flow:

1) Announce the session objective and flow.

2) Review the team mission, vision, and values to clarify and confirm the big picture of what difference the team is making for the stakeholders and for the company.

3) Ask each member to develop and write mid- to long-term (e.g., 2 - 5 years; use appropriate length for your team) achievements/deliverables on a flip-chart by sub-team or individually if owning a solo role; 20 minutes.

4) Stop the work when the time is over and ask each member or sub-team to present

their mid-term achievements/deliverables in conjunction with the team vision and mission; 5 minutes. Ask the rest of the members to write their feedback (positive, concerns or suggestions) and questions in PostIt notes while listening the presentation.

5) When all the presentations are done, ask members to hand out the PostIt notes with feedback to each presenter or sub-group.

6) Ask the team to read the feedback and questions, and then review and modify their achievements/deliverables on the flip-chart; 10 minutes.

7) Ask the team to present their revisions and final thoughts on their mid-term achievements/deliverables and commitment to delivering them.

8) Wrap up and close the meeting with appreciation.

2. Empower members to develop annual goals and work plans individually.

This action is about assisting members to set challenging and exciting goals and creating innovative work plans for the coming year.

As members have already developed their challenging mid- to long-term term achievements, they are in a better position to set the right goals and plans that are challenging and inspiring for them to go after for the coming 12 months. However, a manager still needs to support their effort through conversation to ensure their success.

Goal: All members are clear about and committed to what and how they will achieve this year - inspiring goals and innovative work plans to get there and feeling excited about moving forward.

Action: Announce an annual goal-setting and work planning process and hold a one-on-one meeting individually to agree on each members' annual goals and work plans (physically or online).

Preparation/Materials Needed: None, other than the team mission and vision, and the individuals' mid- to long-term achievement/deliverables set previously.

Example Flow:

1) Announce the goal-setting and work planning process, and ask each member to set inspiring, annual goals and work plans with a target implementation and completion timescale.

    If this is the first time for members to officially plan their goals and key initiatives or work plans, you may want to ask several questions before they start working on their goal-setting. The purpose of asking questions is to enable them to identify their goals and plans from holistic and external perspectives, e.g., market trends, unmet customer needs, internal stakeholder needs, hot technologies and systems available in the market, and so on and so forth. The following are some examples of initial questions you may ask your members.
    (1) How have you set your annual goals and plans in the past?

> (2) What else would you like to do to set inspiring goals and innovative work plans for the coming year?
> (3) What else?
> (4) What are some other things superstar players in your position doing to identify innovative or effective initiatives and plans?

Once the members get the overall picture of how they analyze situations and develop goals and plans, appreciate their effort, encourage their out-of-box thinking, and show your high expectation for their inspiring goals and plans.

2) Ask them to book a one-on-one meeting with their manager for goal and plan alignment.

3) Conduct a one-on-one meeting with each member and align their annual goals and work plans. The leader needs to be supportive for their presented goals and work plans, as no one wants to be rejected. Before giving your feedback or thoughts, ask clarifying questions for better understanding; ask exploring questions to expand their thinking and ideas. Do not

override and impose your own ideas. It will not work - "human beings commit to what they decide and what they say." Imposing goes against "empowering," and it will simply demotivate and discourage your members not to be creative.

Once you and the member are aligned, ask them how they want to have a project review with you - how frequently, how to proceed, what media (face-to-face, online, etc.). Once both of you are aligned, ask them to send in their finalized goals and work plans. Close with appreciation, high expectation, and encouragement.

When you receive the member's confirmation, please appreciate their action and give feedback if needed.

3. Empower members to coordinate and align annual team plans.

Often, members don't know, specifically, what other team members are working on. In high performing teams, members know what other members are working on, and coordinate and collaborate where ever possible, which is what makes them high performing.

This leadership action is empowering members to openly share their goals and work plans in a team meeting to identify coordination and collaboration opportunities. Also, having both team and individuals' goals and plans visible will help members to understand what the team is working on and how each member is contributing individually and collaboratively to achieve the common goal, which will be a source of appreciation.

Goal: All members are clear about what they will be doing individually and collectively and how to coordinate the work to achieve this year's goals.

Please see an example of total team plans in a tree-chart format on the next page. This type of one-page chart will be very helpful for the team to grasp their annual plans and how each member's actions are interrelated and connected to the team strategy.

Action: Hold a team meeting to produce an annual team business plan (and/or projects) that indicates the goals, key dates, and responsible and supporting members' names (Annual project and event calendar).

Preparation/Materials Needed: Wall-paper or whiteboard, color markers, and PostIt notes; Each member needs to prepare their annual goals and work plans/projects in a presentable format (PowerPoint slide or on a flip-chart).

Example Flow:

1) Announce the session objective and flow.

2) Review the team mission, vision, and values to clarify and confirm the big picture of what difference the team is making for the stakeholders and for the company.

3) Ask each member to introduce their annual goals and key projects or work plans over the next 12 months, in conjunction with the team vision and mission. Ask the rest of the members to write feedback (positive, concerns, and suggestions for coordination and collaboration) and questions on PostIt notes while listening the presentation.

4) After each presentation, the presenter invites feedback and suggestions for coordination or collaboration from the rest of

the team. The leader may facilitate the discussion as needed.

5) After all the presentations and discussions are completed, ask the team to indicate their final plans on a wall-paper (or flip-chart or whiteboard).

6) Ask the team to review the team annual plan and confirm their understanding and commitment. Ask the team to send in modified goals and plans if they made any changes or modifications; incorporating the input from and discussion with other members.

7) Wrap up and close the meeting with appreciation. (You may ask the team to give their feedback and questions written on PostIt notes to the right person.)

Team Strategic Planning

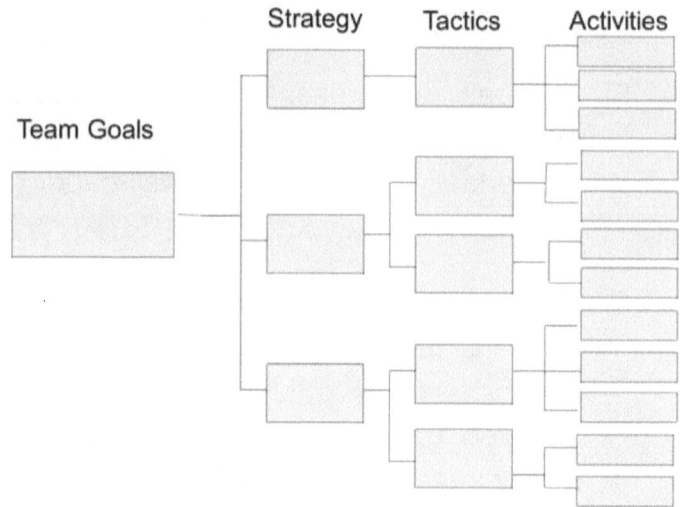

4. Energize members to implement and achieve their work plans.

This is about creating an atmosphere in the team that make the members feel excited, energized, and confident about implementing and achieving their plans and goals. (Of course, the intent of this should not be checking, fault-finding, and pressurizing to members to make them complete their tasks.)

Goal: All members feel excited, energized, and confident about implementing and achieving their plans and goals; their plans and goals are achieved. As they achieved their quick wins, they feel a sense of accomplishment and growth.

Action: The leader encourages, shows excitement, high expectation, and confidence about the members capability and actions to complete their plans and deliver great results. Gives feedback and coaching as appropriate.

Preparation/Materials Needed: None

Example Activities/Behaviors:

1) Always stay in a positive and energetic mode in front of members.

2) Give appreciation and positive comments.

3) Ask questions about their key initiatives.

4) When hearing positive feedback about member's achievements, praise their wins and let other members know.

5) During a progress review meeting, actively listen to what members say about their goals, actions, results, and reflection. Stay positive, show your interest in their work, and ask questions to learn more about their work and achievements, so

that the members feel further excited about continuing great work with their best effort.

5. Celebrate members achievements.

People want to be recognized and praised when they have made a great effort and done a great job; they will be further excited when their efforts and accomplishments are celebrated. The team's celebration could also be a great opportunity for the team to learn together, reapply others' success factors, and further expand the successes in the team.

Goal: All members feel good about their own achievements, be clear about key factors for others success, and energized about reapplying those success factors to their own projects or work.

Action: Hold a team meeting to announce and celebrate the success in the team and share any learnings from the success. This could be held on a monthly or quarterly basis.

Preparation/Materials Needed: snacks and drinks, gift if appropriate or needed

Example Flow:

1) Opening remark.

2) Announce the success and big achievements of the team.

3) Ask for a presentation in a STAR format from those who made the success - situation of the business, task to do, key actions taken, and results from their action with some reflective comments, such as success factors and future improvement opportunities.

4) Celebrate the success and recap the highlights of the success.

5) Ask each member to think and share with neighbors their takeaways from the successes introduced.

6) Close the session with appreciation, excitement, encouragement, and high expectation for further success for the next month/quarter.

In Summary

Top-down goal-setting and planning are sure ways to discourage and demotivate the team. Autonomy and self-directedness will be key drivers for engaging, motivating and energizing the team to do their best to achieve the team mission and vision. The leader will promote true empowerment through putting members in the driver's seat, so that they take ownership to analyze, plan, implement, reflect, and achieve their mission. In so doing, the entire team will align and united toward achieving the common direction collaboratively. The additional benefit of "empowering" is to energize the whole team to get excited about bringing the best out of the members to achieve their peak performance.

The leader's important job is truly delegating to the team to create and deliver the plans individually and collaboratively, while respecting, trusting, and supporting each member throughout this whole empowering process. (Please see dos and don'ts of empowering leadership in the below chart.)

Dos and Don'ts of leaders in Empowering

Dos	Don'ts
• Respect and trust each and everyone in the team • Fully and truly delegate • Stay energetic, excited, and positive • Show high expectation • Be accessible • Energize the team to deliver expected outcomes • Create alignment, co-learning, and celebration opportunities • Give feedback and coaching whenever needed	• Be skeptical about member's capability • Delegate partially • Stay lukewarm, indifferent, and pessimistic • Fail to express your expectation • Be hands-free, Laissez-Faire • Be unexcited about member's efforts and achievements • Fail to connect the team to align, learn together, and celebrate • Be unsupportive when members need feedback and support

Chapter 7

Leadership Action 4 - Enable Members

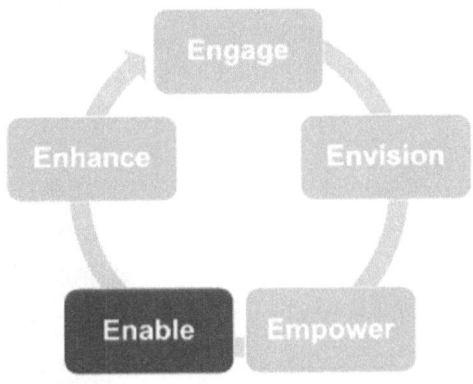

"Enabling Members" Leadership

In the last three chapters, we discussed "how to engage" members and build a trusting community, "how to envision" to inspire members to get excited about creating an ideal future, and "how to empower" members to get energized around developing and executing team plans. What more do leaders need to do to orchestrate the team to achieve the team mission and vision?

As the team is now aspiring to a challenging, yet meaningful, vision, members need to upgrade their competency, to execute innovative ideas and plans they have never done before. So, in this Chapter, we will discuss how we, as leaders, can best enable our members so that they will fully utilize their potential and complete their challenging yet meaningful tasks.

First, let's look at the key elements for the human growth.

We have all had several growth periods during our work life. In such a time, we feel, "I grew a lot as a professional, and I can confidently perform my role and deliver expected results all by myself." Please remember a few periods you felt like that.

In those growth periods, what kind of work did you work on? What did you accomplish? How were you tackling the work? Who were you working with? What challenges did you experience over the course? How did you overcome those challenges and struggles? Who helped you achieve that?

Reflecting some of your growth experiences and responding those questions, what do you think are some of the important factors for your growth as a professional? Please write down your important growth accelerating factors in below column.

My Growth Accelerators:

1.

2.

3.

I have asked these questions to thousands of managers in the past, and I almost always got very similar responses from them. The most frequently mentioned growth factors are the following:

  1) Challenging work - the work I have never done by myself before; difficult problems

my customer gave me, and I struggled and solved the problem by myself; my boss suddenly left the company, and I was tasked to complete his job by myself; I was assigned to work with difficult customers, and I learned a lot about how to understand and satisfy their real needs.

2) New environment and/or role - I changed companies (or I moved to a new country) and worked with people with different practices, values, and logic, and I needed to broaden my perspectives and work styles to deliver the results; I became a manager, and I needed to manage some difficult members.

3) Boss and coach - I learned lots of new ways of solving problems from my boss while I was working with her; I had a good advice and coaching from my boss, especially when I was stuck and couldn't move forward; my boss encouraged me to take a risk and try something new, and that helped me see the new horizon and grow fast.

You might have thought of some of the above factors as your growth accelerating factors. The above growth factors are consistent with the findings by the Center for Creative Leadership who indicate 70% of learning comes from challenging work experience, 20% comes from the boss, and 10% comes from learning and development experience, including self-study.

So, as a leader, the best way to help members grow is to assign them to challenging and meaningful work. This can be done by "empowering," where the leader assist members to identify some challenging, important, and meaningful tasks to achieve the team mission and vision. If the leader does the right job in "empowering," members should be working on challenging assignments and projects with strong ownership. So they must be well engaged and motivated to accomplish their tasks. (We discussed this topic in the prior Chapter - "Empowering" leadership.) That covers the 70% of the growth of members.

This Chapter will focus more on the rest of 30% of the human growth - what leaders should personally do to help the member grow further.

As the change is constant, we all need to continuously learn and grow our capacity and capability to satisfy ever-changing customer needs better than our competitors. Leaders of high-performance teams are enablers – they support their members to develop their competencies and commitment to become true professionals who can consistently deliver the desired results.

As indicated in the first Chapter, the team performance will be dependent on an individual's competency (or ability and knowledge) and commitment (or motivation, mindset, and emotional state), and context (leader, team members, process, system, artifacts, and culture). This Chapter will show several effective leadership actions to help members advance and strengthen their capability and mindset, and therefore, improve their performance.

> Performance = Competency x Commitment x Context

What: "Enabling" is about enhancing members skillsets (competency) and mindset (commitment) through various actions and methods, such as giving feedback, offering training, and coaching to further advance their performance.

Why: As research by the Center for Creative Leadership indicates, the leader is one of key growth accelerating factors (McCauley, Moxley and Van Velsor). Their enabling actions will not only help members become better performers but also become more motivated and committed to further excel their performance.

A Gallup research among employees has revealed the following (https://www.gallup.com/workplace/231620/why-performance-development-wins-workplace.aspx):

- 30% of employees strongly agree that their manager involves them in goal-setting
- 27% strongly agree the feedback they receive helps them do their work better
- 22% strongly agree their performance is managed in a way that motivates them
- 19% strongly say that they talked to their manager about steps to reach their goals

The above data indicates leaders need to do a better job in terms of (a) setting and aligning clear goals, (b) providing timely feedback, and (c) supporting their development.

See the below chart indicating typical characteristics of the team with and without "Enabling Members."

Characteristics of the team with and without "Enabling Members."

Team Characteristics "with Enabling Members"	Team Characteristics "without Enabling Members"
• Members are self-learners	• Members don't learn new things
• Less reliant on the manager	• Reliant on the manager
• Able to think from broad perspectives	• Think mostly from own perspectives
• Continue to increase networking and thinking agility	• Doesn't expand network or change thinking pattern
• Try something new continuously	• Always do the same things
• Make improvements constantly	• Maintains current practices
• Actively listens to others	• Doesn't listen carefully
• Learning is taking place in the whole team	• Not much learning taking place in the team

Key Areas for Leaders to Build Members Performance

1. Support members to identify their professional goal.

We have already discussed how to align the work goals. I'd like to discuss how leaders align members professional goals, as this is often not thoroughly discussed between the leader and members.

Example Goal-setting Action

Support Members to Identify their Professional Goal.

Holding an inspiring goal is very effective in keeping us moving forward, despite hardship, as it will give us hope, courage, and resiliency, working as a source of motivation. Members of high-performance teams usually have a personal vision, their ideal future state that they want to strive for along with their inspiring team vision. A personal vision can help members identify how they can get there - what skill set and mindset they need to strengthen or acquire, and how to do those in both short- and long-term.

Goal: All members are clear about and committed to achieving their long-term professional visions prior to the short-term one.

Action: Hold one-on-one meetings with each member to help develop their professional vision or ideal future state primarily through asking questions; 1 - 1.5 hour per member.

Preparation/Materials Needed: Individual's mid-term achievement.

Example Questions During the Meeting:

a) Who are your ideal professionals in this field?
b) Why are they ideal? What have they achieved?
c) What attributes and capability do you like about them?
d) What kind of mindset do they possess to help them make those achievements?
e) Suppose this is 5 years from now, and you have already become your ideal professional that is parity or even surpassing those ideal professionals you just mentioned. What have you achieved in the last 5 years?

f) For you to make those achievements, what skills have you strengthened or gained in the last 5 years?
g) For you to make those achievements, what are your inner strengths or mindset you strengthened or built in the last 5 years?
h) If we extend the time line from 5 to 10 years, what other achievements do you wish to add? What other skill set do you want to possess? What other mindset do you include?
i) So that we are clear, can you please summarize your ideal future vision?
j) Imagine we are still 5 years from today, and you've already achieved your personal vision and made lots of achievements. The company selected you as the most valuable contributor of the year, and you are at the ceremony, surrounded by senior executives, colleagues, and customers. What are they saying about you? How about the company president? How about your members? How about peers? How about customers? And, how do you feel?

Hint for Successful Long-term Professional Goal-Setting:

1) Open-ended questions - Ask lots of open-ended questions to help members think through, expand their horizon, and self-determine their ideal vision. Do not instill your ideas, as that will hinder member's ownership and creativity.

2) Active listening - Focus your attention on your members, and actively listen to them. Acknowledge their thoughts and emotions, even though you may not agree.

3) SMART goals – Help them make their goals specific (S), measurable (M), achievable (A), relevant (R), and time bound (T). Vague, unclear goals will not likely be achieved, and goals without measurement will be difficult to track their progress.

4) Inspiring – Help them make their goals inspiring and exciting. If the goal is dull and unchallenging, members will not be motivated to achieve it.

5) In case you don't agree with what members say, first, acknowledge their thinking and effort, and then, ask what-if questions or reframing questions to help members expand their thinking or look from a broader or different perspective.

2. Giving feedback.

Bosses' feedback is critical for members to understand their performance and progress and correct or redirect the course as necessary. Good feedback can help members understand how they are doing, where they are, and get them motivated to further strengthen their strong capability or improve their weak areas.

What feedback have you given your members in the last 7 days? How did that feedback land on members? What new behaviors did your members exhibit after your feedback? How did their behavioral changes impact their performance and results?

If your responses to the above questions are all positive, you must be doing a great job in giving feedback to your members! So, please, keep it up.

Most managers have a preference or a default mode when it comes to giving feedback. Some managers have tendency to focus on members' good points and often give praise and positive feedback, some other managers tend to find members' faults and give negative feedback. Yet other managers care less about members' work and performance, so don't give much feedback to them. Which one among the three is your usual mode? Which mode do you think is most effective to improve members' behaviors and performance?

Research by Gallup on the impact of different types of feedback indicates a correlation between those three modes of manager's feedback and the behavioral changes of those who received the feedback (https://www.learnevents.com/blog/2014/09/25/positive-negative-or-no-feedback-at-all/). The most effective mode is giving positive feedback that improves members' performance consistently over time. Giving negative feedback tends to be effective in changing members' behaviors initially but becomes ineffective as it continues over and over. The least impactful one is giving no feedback, as members do not understand how they are doing. Positive feedback helps increase members' self-efficacy as well as their trust in the leader.

Another type of feedback is constructive feedback, where managers give feedback on improvement areas to members in a way that is understandable to members, maintaining their self-esteem. So, leaders need to learn when and how to give positive and constructive feedback in a most effective manner to improve members' performance.

Example Feedback Actions:

1) Giving Positive Feedback

Goal: All members are clear about their current performance and strengths, and they are committed to expanding the use of their strengths to maximize results.

Action: Hold a one-on-one conversation with each member to give positive feedback; 2 - 3 minutes.

Flow: Situation – Behaviors – Impact – Close.

    (1) **Situation -** Opening remark that indicates the situation with a positive tone e.g.,

"Thank you for the great work at today's promotion event for our new product!"

(2) **Behaviors that were good** - Tell them your perspective on their positive aspects and specific strengths that the member has exhibited to make it happen. e.g., *"It was really good that you had customers experience our products that we never did before rather than just showing our product demo. Your customer centric strengths and trying something new really worked."*

(3) **Impact** - Tell them the impact on the business and/or the team and how you felt about that. *"As a result, we were able to close 20 deals on the spot - already made $500,000! I am very happy and proud of your talent, and the lots of effort you have put into this event."*

(4) **Close** - Close the conversation with Appreciating their ideas, encourage and show high expectation for their keeping it up. e.g., *"Again, thank you for the great work. I continue to count on your innovative work. Keep it up."*

2) Giving Constructive Feedback

Goal: All members are clear about their current performance and next steps to strengthen their performance, and they are committed to do so.

Action: Hold one-on-one meetings with each member to give positive feedback; 3 - 5 minutes.

Flow: Situation – member's perspectives – your perspectives – their indicated action - close

(1) **Situation** - Opening remark that indicates the situation with a positive remark and tone, e.g., *"Thank you for the lots of effort you put in for today's promotion event for our new product."*

(2) **Their perspective** - Ask for their perspective before you indicate your thinking. e.g., *"How do you think the event was for the participants?"*

(3) **Your perspective** - Indicate your perspective
   i. Acknowledge - First, acknowledge their perspective. e.g., *"Yes, your promotion has generated lots of in-*

terest, and we achieved our target of 500 visitors today."

ii. Good points - Add your comments on positive aspects and specific strengths the member has exhibited to make it happen. e.g., *"It was really good that you had customers experienced our products, and they got really excited about what they saw. Your strengths of trying something new really worked."*

iii. Improvement points - State neutrally your perspective on improvement areas. e.g., *"I saw those who experienced our product's benefits leave our booth with none of our sales people following up, as many were busy with pitching to prospects around our booth. I see that as our opportunity lost, and we could do better."*

(4) **Their indicated actions** - Ask for their ideas to improve the performance or solve the problem. e.g., *"If you had the same opportunity again, what would you do differently to do even greater job?"*

(5) **Close** - Appreciate their ideas, encourage and show high expectation for their keeping it up. e.g., *"That would work! Again, thank you for the good effort. I have a high expectation of your work and your trying-something-new attitude. Keep it up."*

Hints for Successful Feedback:

1) Behavior focus - Describe specific behaviors that are good and to be continued or bad that need to be improved. Members do not understand if the leader makes comment on their attitudes or personality.

2) Timeliness - Give feedback on the spot or within a day or so when their memory is fresh. Poor leaders accumulate feedback on different occasions and discuss them all at once. It's not only ineffective, but also a sure way to lose credibility and trust from members.

3) Balanced - Give balanced feedback. Even when members made mistakes, they have usually done something good on that work or project. So, it's better that we give positive feedback. Focus your atten-

tion on your members, and actively listen to them.

4) Focused - Give focused feedback. People cannot remember so many things at a time. So, please focus your feedback only on one or two make-or-break behaviors.

5) Positive intent - Always give a positive stroke with a positive intent. Don't make your feedback explode with your anger or frustration. Feedback with negative emotion will usually have a negative impact on member's emotion and productivity.

6) Clear indicated action - Be sure that members are clear about their indicated actions after the feedback conversation is over. Otherwise, your feedback time and effort may not bear any fruit on member's behaviors or performance.

3. Coaching.

Coaching is a type of conversation between a manager and a member that helps the member grow and perform better. What is your typical conversation with your members at the workplace? What is the focus of your conversation?

Who is talking more, you or members? When you speak, do you spend time more on telling or more on listening? How are the members engaged in the conversation - proactive and positive or passive and quiet? How does your conversation usually end - positive and aligned or neutral or misaligned?

Modern coaching practices became popular the in 1980s in various fields, such as sports coaching, business coaching, executive coaching, and life coaching. The International Coaches Federation defines "Coaching is partnering with clients in a thought-provoking and creative process that inspires them to maximize their personal and professional potential."

In a coaching conversation in a work setting, managers talk with members to provoke their thoughts to maximize their potential and performance. Important skills used in coaching to provoke members thoughts are questioning and listening. Powerful questioning and active listening will help members understand how they are doing currently, identify what they want to achieve or who they want to be, and determine specifically how they will go about getting there.

Members expand their thinking during a coaching conversation, broaden their perspectives and make decisions, and then, start taking new actions and behaviors. What is more, it is this thinking and acting processes that are very important for their learning and growth. Brain science studies revealed that when we think or experience something new, our brain gets activated and changes form, increasing our thinking and acting capacity (https://www.ncbi.nlm.nih.gov/pmc/articles/PMC3222570/). This is because our brain is made up of billions of brain cells, or neurons; when we think or do something new or different, our brain cells make new connections with other brain cells that we haven't used before, using more parts of brain.

Going back to the prior question on your current conversation with your members, how well are you currently using powerful questions to help members provoke their thinking and expand their perspectives? How actively are you listening to what members are saying? The better you listen, the more the members speak what they are thinking, feeling, and experiencing.

Case Example

A manufacturing organization of an electronic company conducted employee opinion survey and identified several issues in the organization. As one of their main problems was employee engagement and a poor rating of their managers, the manufacturing plant has implemented coaching training for managers to learn how to empower and help members grow and perform better.

All the managers on the site have learned basic coaching skills as well as fundamental people development skills and mindsets through a series of role plays with peers. Each participating manager has developed action plans to immediately implement at their workplace and have since implemented their plans.

Several weeks after the workshop, the plant HR manager started hearing positive comments from employees. Their employee opinion survey in the following year indicated significantly improved scores on "managers' effectiveness," up by more than 30%. Similarly, the members' engagement scores also increased by more than 30%. It simply proved the positive impact of managers' coaching or enabling skills and behaviors. The survey data also indicated enhanced work processes and improved overall communication at the plant while there were no other change initiatives at this plant in that period. This was one of my earlier successes in offering a coaching program to build a coaching and development culture in organizations.

Example Coaching Action

1) GROW coaching

The GROW coaching model is a useful tool, especially for members who are starting a new position or new project or even reframing an existing task. GROW is an acronym - G stands for "Goal," R stand for "Reality," O stands for "Options," and W stands for "Will or Way forward." GROW coaching conversation starts with setting a meaningful goal with a growth mindset rather than analyzing current situations or issues with a fault-finding mentality. Our brain gets more excited and innovative when we think about a bright future. The GROW model can certainly be used for those who get stuck with their project and need some fresh perspective to move forward.

Goal: Members are clear about their goals, current status, options to achieve their goals, and specific next step(s); the members are also committed to achieving the goals.

Action: Hold a one-on-one coaching conversation with each member to help develop their goal and plans, primarily through powerful questions and active listening; 5 - 30 minutes per session.

Preparation/Materials Needed: Agreed work plans or development plans of members — if needed. If you are not used to doing coaching conversation, it's always good to prepare sufficient powerful questions prior to the session and rehearse beforehand.

Example GROW Coaching Flow

(1) **Goal** - Ask powerful questions to help members set inspiring goals. Example questions:
- *"What kind of goals would make you feel great if achieved?"*
- *"For you to achieve that goal, specifically what competency do you need?"*
- *"What would be the ideal mindset you need to achieve that goal?"*

- "How would you feel when you have achieved that goal?"

(2) **Reality** - Ask powerful questions to help members identify where they are versus their goals. Example questions:
- "Against your goal, where are you now on this project?"
- "How confident are you in achieving your goal?"
- "What is the reason for that level of confidence?"
- Against the competency required to attain the goal, where are you?"
- What do you need to add to your competency repertoire mindset to achieve that goal?"

(3) **Options** - Ask powerful questions to help members develop as many options as possible to achieve their goals. Example questions:
- "What do you want to do to close the gap between your goals and the current status?"
- "What resources in our company can you use to attain your goal?"

- *"What actions have you seen in the marketplace in achieving this kind of goal?"*
- *"What technologies are our key competitor utilizing in this effort?"*
- *"Among the options you have just created, which ones are your top 3?"* *"Which one is your number 1 action?"*

(4) **Way forward** - Ask powerful questions to help members determine specific next actions to make a positive move toward achieving their goals. Please note that their next steps are about their most effective option that they selected at the end of "Option" conversation. Example questions:
- *"For you to move your number action forward, what do you want to do this week?"*
- *"When do you want to make it happen?"*
- *"Then, when should we meet again to review your progress?"*

2) Reflective coaching

Reflective coaching is very useful for any members.

Goal: Members are clear about the current status of the work or project and specific next step(s) to achieve the goal.

Action: Hold one-on-one coaching conversations with each member to help develop their goal and plans, primarily through powerful question and active listening; 5 - 30 minutes per member.

Preparation/Materials Needed: Agreed work plans or development plans of members if needed. If you are not used to doing coaching conversation, it's always good to prepare sufficient powerful questions prior to the session.

Example Reflection Coaching Flow

- (1) **Target** - Ask for a recap of target goals and plans. Example questions:
    - *"What were your targets?"*
    - *"What were intended value-adds for your stakeholders?"*

(2) **Wins** - Ask for successes they achieved. Example questions:
- "What went as well as you planned"
- "What feedback did you get?"
- "What were the factors for that success?"

(3) **Challenge** - Ask for their challenges. Example questions:
- "What did not go as well as you planned?
- What feedback did you get?"
- "What made it difficult to achieve?"

(4) **Opportunity** - Ask for new opportunities and possibilities. Example questions:
- "What changes or emerging trends are you seeing in the market (client, competitors, stakeholders, partners, technologies, environment)?"
- "What possibilities and opportunities do you see in this situation?"

(5) **Action** - Ask for the next steps to achieve goals. Example questions:
- "Knowing those challenges, what are you going to do to hit your target?"

- *"To capitalize those opportunities and achieve your goals, what do you want to do?"*

(6) **Reflection** - Ask for their learning. Example questions:
- *"Reflecting on this experience, what did you learn?*
- *"How do you want to further grow from this experience?"*

"GROW" Model Framework

G	**Goal:** To develop specific and inspiring goals by asking about: • Target results • The significance of those results • Skill set needed to achieve those results • Mindset needed • Key stakeholders • How to ascertain the success • Their emotions when achieved
R	**Reality:** To ascertain current realities by asking about: • Current results • Current skill set • Current mindset

	• Current stakeholders and their perspectives • Self-evaluations on current situations
O	**Options:** To develop as many alternative ideas to achieve the above goal as possible from various perspectives, such as: • Available resources • Benchmarking • Customer and competitors' perspectives • Disruptive innovations • Experts' practices • What-if scenarios
W	**Way Forward:** To determine specific next steps on the most promising option from the above brainstorming by asking about: • The most impactful idea from all the options • Actions to be taken around that idea within a week • Date and time to take those actions • When to meet to discuss the outcomes from taking those actions

Hint for Successful Coaching:

1) Members accountability - Always have members in the driver's seat to keep their ownership and accountability. Do not give your own answer, which will discourage and demotivate your members.

2) Powerful questions - Ask many powerful questions to help members think from different angles and expand their horizon. Limit closed-ended or leading questions, as that will not enhance members thinking power.

3) Be curious - Be interested and inquisitive about your members and their thoughts, feelings, and actions. If you become interested about learning about your members, you will have lots of questions when talking with them.

4) Trust your members - Trust members' thinking power and capability for solving problems or grasping opportunities. If you trust them, it shows in your attitudes, language, and facial expressions, and creates a psychologically safe and resourceful space.

5) Be patient - Don't speak when members are quiet or thinking, as that will distract their train of thoughts as well as discouraging their ownership. This may not be easy for many people, especially for those who are uncomfortable about having a long silence moment.

4. Teaching.

While coaching is effective for those who have some experience or knowledge about the topic, teaching is needed and effective for those with no experience or knowledge on the topic. So, depending on the level of knowledge and experience, leaders need to identify when and what to teach or coach for each of their members.

Just like teachers teach students theories, approaches, formula, and models in school, managers need to teach newcomers in key theories, guiding principles, problem-solving approaches, or formula, so that they can learn to perform their task effectively.

In high-performance teams, leaders teach inexperienced members in fundamental business and communication skills in addition to technical competency, regardless of their experience levels. For example, when my first company was acquired, the parent company offered us a fundamental communication program, so that we could effectively and efficiently communicate in the new business environment where there was a specific communication method, e.g., all the documents needed to be made within one page, and there was a specific writing structure and format to help readers understand and make decisions quickly. It was a truly needed learning opportunity for me.

Many leaders do not offer much learning opportunity for mid-career hires, assuming they are supposed to be equipped with all the technical skills, which is not likely! I have seen many sales organizations with lots of mid-career hires who do not teach selling process and skills. In such organizations, sales activities and processes vary by individual. Many sales professionals keep using the same process and techniques they learned from their managers early in their career. The fact of the matter is that companies where all members understand and implement best practices, they consistently outsell over those who don't have that practice. The Brooks Group, a US-based sales training consulting company indicates organizations with a consistent sales process close deals twice as much as those who don't.

Keys to Effective Teaching and Learning Experience

When you are assigned to a new job or project, what do you usually do to gain the new expertise? Learn from the manual? Observe other's actions? Learn from the expert?

Our preferred learning styles are different from individual to individual, and there are four basic learning styles.

a) Theory-oriented – This type of person wants to learn the theory and logic behind new skills first or before they actually try something new.

b) Observation-oriented - This type of person wants to observe other people doing the task before they perform.

c) Action-oriented - This type of person just wants to get on and try the new skill or task themselves. They want to learn by doing.

d) Heart-oriented - This type of person wants to feel the meaning of learning the new skill and task.

As there are different learning styles or preferences, we involve those four elements when teaching people - learning logic, observing good examples, demonstrate, applying new skills, and consolidating the skills through feedback.

Telling is not teaching. Teaching is involving members in a learning experience. Good leaders will help members learn by head, heart, and hand, or intellectually, emotionally, and physically so that members can reapply the newly learned skills and tasks effectively and correctly time after time.

Case Example

A construction company K had been continuously experiencing poor retention of new employees and losing more than half of newly hired people within one year.

The owner of the company, as he was old and suffering from heart disease, decided to call his son to replace him to become the leader of the company. His son thought about it for some days, and he finally decided to join the company and became the new head of the company. As he talked with existing members, he understood the quality of the service was very good, but he identified a poor retention of new employees as the key area to improve as a top priority.

The existing practice of a new employee induction program was a 3-day company orientation program to teach the industry, the company history, and also, what they needed to do. After this orientation, new hires were sent out to the construction site to work with existing members and a supervisor. The new leader interviewed recent hires as well as those who were hired in the last several years, and he learned that they really struggled right after they were sent to work with other members as they had not learned many necessary skills and were forced to learn by observing and learning from other members. They were frustrated as they couldn't perform well and gained no recognition or positive feedback at the workplace.

The new leader decided to change the existing practice and implemented a month-long program for new employees to master the skills before going out to the construction site. He offered the learning program using an "explain-demonstrate-apply-consolidate" cycle for the first few days. Then, new employees started practicing on their own, using video as instructed in the curriculum without further teaching. More specifically, all newcomers watched a video showing a master's practice and skills. They practiced the skill to work like a master. At the same time, they filmed their own practice using their smart phone, and after the practice, they watched their actions, comparing them with a master's action. They soon started self-correcting their actions and skills. Importantly, they were motivated to master the skills, as they could see how they were growing their skills from watching their videos.

After completing a new learning program, they are sent to the real workplace to demonstrate their competency. Now newcomers are engaged with the work as they can perform the task on the day they were sent, and colleagues recognize their performance. Since this new learning program started, no new employees have left the company – marvelous results started by the leader!

Goal: All members can perform the new skill and task effectively and correctly.

Action/Flow: Give learning experience as either one-on-one or in a group setting for them to learn and practice a new task and/or skill.

Preparation/Materials Needed: Task or process sheet or skill-list if needed.

Sample Teaching Flow

1) **Explain** - Explain what members will learn, why they need to learn, and how they will learn. e.g., *"Today you will learn ... skill. This skill is important when you... It will also be necessary if you want to advance your career to the next level. The flow of this learning session is ..."*

2) **Demonstrate** - Leaders need to demonstrate the right example of performing the new task or skill. Before demonstrating, describe the basic process or steps to perform the task. While demonstrating the task, explain specifically what you are doing and why that is important. It's always good if you explain key theory, principles, and success factors with good and bad examples. E.g., *"This task can be broken into 4 parts – first..., second..., third...*

and fourth... I will demonstrate one by one. In the first part, we do... we do this because ... (theory). Key point in this part is... Watch-out is... So, a good example is... A bad example is... Any questions? If no questions, let me move on to the second part... (Repeat this pattern until you complete your demonstration of all the task and skill.)"

3) **Apply** - Ask members to actually do the task or skill to show their understanding and learning. e.g., *"Now please try for yourself what you have just observed and learned. Now I want you to demonstrate your newly learned task. Who wants to go first?"*

4) **Consolidate** - Appreciate members trial and good effort and give feedback to consolidate their learning. Before giving feedback, ask for their comments on their performance. If you think they need to change or improve the skill or performance, ask questions on the point to be changed, so that you can check their understanding of the skills and knowledge. Then, provide your feedback and ask for

their retrial. If they have done a perfect performance, acknowledge, appreciate, and congratulate them on their great performance. State your high expectation on when and how to use the newly learned skill. Before closing the session, check and confirm when they will use the newly learned skills.

Effective Teaching Cycle

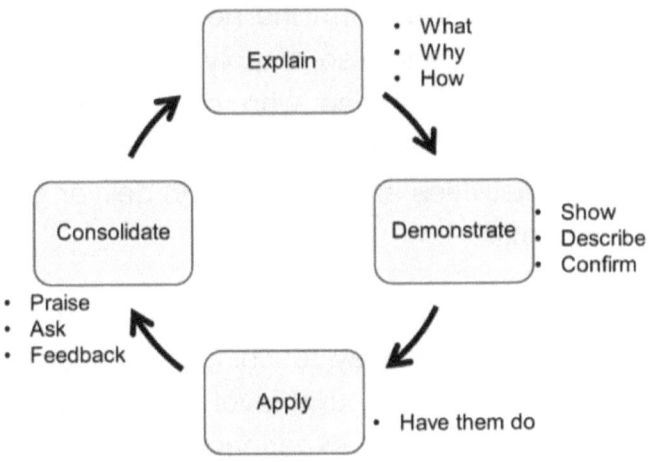

Hint for Successful Teaching:

1) Clarify meaning - Make sure members understand why they need to learn the skill and how that will help them grow and perform better before starting to teach them. If the members see the clear link

between the new skill and their future performance or advanced competency and responsibility, they will be fired up to learn the new skill.

2) Logic and reasoning - Teach not only the skill but also the core theory, principles, and evidence behind the process, skills, and mindset. If they understand the logic behind their actions or behaviors, they can likely perform the newly learned skill correctly and also reapply it in a variety of situations. Those who often make mistakes usually don't know why certain skills or activities are necessary to deliver great results.

3) Involve learners in lots of learning experience – One-way teaching seldom works. Make it 2-way, and involve the members in the learning experience, such as having them observe how you perform the skill or task, making them demonstrate their learning, asking questions to enhancer their understanding. The more you involve them, the better they remember and perform the new skill and task.

4) Immediate reapplication on the job – Have members demonstrate their new skills on the job as soon as possible. Learning should happen right before the actual performance on the job. If the newly learned skills are not used on the job soon enough, members will likely forget exactly how do the task or use the skill they learned.

5) Follow-up – Follow-up, ask and confirm their progress. If they learn important skills or mindset, "inspect what you expect" to ensure members are fully capable and confident about performing the learned skill and task. It' also good to ask them to report back their progress and achievements to the rest of the team members.

So, leaders need to effectively use both coaching and teaching for helping members grow, depending on the experience level of members. Please see a chart on the next page to clarify how to use teaching and coaching effectively.

Summary of "Teaching" versus "Coaching"

	Teaching	Coaching
WHEN	Leaners have no experiences of the topic you are teaching – they have not even seen or heard.	Leaners have some experiences of the topic you are coaching – they have tried fully or partially, or they haven't done themselves but experienced or seen.
WHY	To learn gain new competency • Knowledge • Skills • Processes • Attitudes/mindsets	To strengthen or improve existing competency
HOW	• Tell what to do, why and how to do those • Demonstrate • Have them apply new skills • Praise and consolidate	• Ask open-ended questions to expand learners' perspectives. • Ask open-ended questions to explore new ideas • Confirm their next steps

5. Supporting members learning and development

As indicated by the Center for Creative Leadership research, 10% of learning and growth come from reading, self-study, and participating in training and seminars. Leaders can support members self-development to bring out their full potential.

Goal: All members are motivated to develop themselves and grow their performance.

Example Actions:

1) Allowing learning opportunity – As each member has their own developmental goals and action plans in order for them to be able to achieve their challenging business goals, leaders must support their learning by allowing them to participate in training to develop their necessary skills for the job. As an allocated budget might be limited, leaders need to ensure members (1) identify and focus on the top priority learning and development objectives, (2) set clear measurement, and (3) have clear learning plans.

   This will be part of opportunities leaders offer coaching for members to accelerate their growth. In so doing, you can also do "practice" coaching, where you help them demonstrate their newly learned skills in front of you, so you can give feedback and coaching to consolidate their skills.

2) Learning sharing opportunity – This is to help members present their showcase to the rest of the team.

Our learning sticks when we practice, apply on the job, reflect, and then present and teach other people. So, a leader's job is to help members increase those opportunities. Team meetings will be a great opportunity for members to present their new practice and learning from those new experiences. In so doing, the presenting member will deepen their learning, and other members will also learn from his or her learning.

Key Principles of Good Empowering

1) **Active conversation between manager and members** – As the leader provides feedback and coaching timely in a motivating and encouraging manner (beyond psychologically safe environment), members are truly engaged in the conversation with the leader to make things move forward.

2) **Members' ownership** – As the leader primarily uses a questioning approach, rather than a telling and ordering approach, members are constantly in the driver's seat to think through, make decisions,

take actions, reflect back to make further improvements, and achieve or overachieve their goals.

3) **Continuous learning, improvements, and new trials** – As a byproduct of a coaching conversation with the leader, members are more proactively learning new things and expanding their network even outside of the company to increase their capability and capacity. As a result, they continuously try something new and make improvements.

4) **Leaders are good learners** – In a truly empowered team, there is an exemplary leader who role models proactive learning and continuous improvements. Members model their role model - just like children model what their parents do, not what they say. As mentioned before, great leaders are great learners, especially in this fast-moving, global economy.

In Summary

Leaders are responsible for helping members grow their personal and professional skills and mindset. Leaders' enabling actions include long-term goal-setting, giving feedback, coaching, teaching, and supporting members' self-development. Helping members set their long-term goals will help them set a clear, inspiring personal vision, which will enable them to have a broad perspective on their self-development - a great starting point for making them passionate about self-development.

Giving effective feedback will help members see where they are in their self-development journey, what's working, and what needs to be further developed, just like a health check. Leaders' effective coaching will not only help members grow and strengthen their performance, but also enhance their self-awareness, self-correction, and self-development skills. As no one is perfect, teaching is also a very necessary action to help members build technical expertise as well as personal capability. Lastly, leaders can further support members' self-development through maximizing their opportunity for practicing and demonstrating new skills and presenting their showcases to the entire team.

Empowerment Growth Cycle

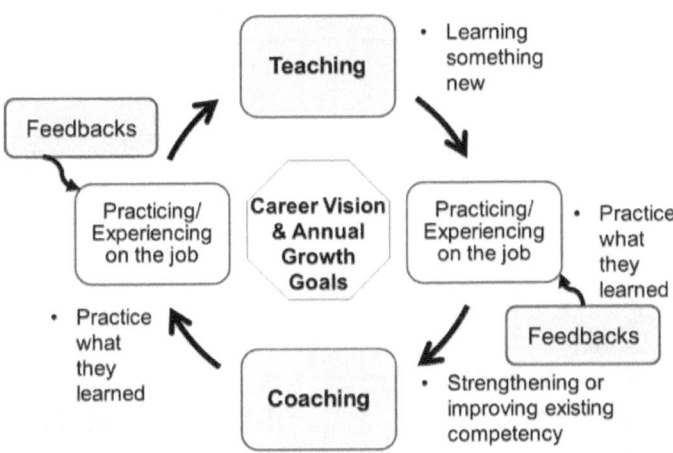

Please check below chart to see how you are currently helping the team to better able to perform better continuously.

Dos and Don'ts of Leaders when Enabling

Dos	Don'ts
• Learn from any opportunities • Learn even from new members • Actively practice new skills • Periodically unlearn old stuff • Be enthusiastic about helping members grow • Help members identify higher self and set higher development goals • Encourage members to take a calculated risk • Give coaching and teaching effectively at the right moment • Focus more on giving positive feedback	• Do not learn • Do not learn from new members • Not interested in new skills • Keep using the same skills • Be indifferent about helping members grow • Leave members alone when they don't have development goals • Keep members only taking conventional skills and approach • Don't give coaching or teaching sufficiently or effectively • Give negative feedback more than positive ones

Chapter 8

Leaders Action 5 - Enhance Systems and Environment

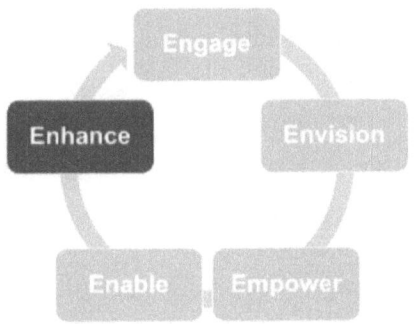

"Enhancing Systems and Environment" Leadership

In the last four chapters, we discussed "how to engage" members and build a trusting community, "how to envision" to inspire members to get excited about creating the ideal future, "how to empower" members to get energized around executing team plans, and "how to enable members" to best help them maximize their capability and capacity. What more do leaders need to do to orchestrate the team to achieve the team mission and vision?

> "All organizations are perfectly designed to get the results they get"

Yes, as discussed in the second Chapter, leaders need to build and strengthen the environment and systems in the team, so that all members will become able to collaborate and deliver results efficiently and flawlessly. David Jones beautifully articulated the importance of strengthening the work process and system (Hanna, 1988), as follows:

What: "Enhancing the environment and systems" is about building effective, efficient, and user-friendly work systems and environment.

Why: If we improve the work processes and systems, we will be able to improve the team performance by enhancing the quality of products and services, and the efficiency and productivity of the team.

Key Output from Enhancing Systems & Environment:

1. **Improved work processes and systems to increase productivity and efficiency** - As indicated by Dr. Deming, the Total Quality Management guru, if we improve our work processes and systems, we can not only eliminate systemic failures but also enhance the team's performance and output. Key focus areas are the followings.

    1) **Core planning system** - This is about how we set goals, develop team strategies and plans, and deploy strategic team plans to achieve the goals.

        Poor performing teams do not have a robust planning system. Key symptoms of those teams are unmet goals, lots of sudden changes in the plan, lots of meetings, unproductive meetings without clear decisions, and uncommitted members.

        In contrast, high-performance teams have a solid goal-setting and strategic planning process that involves members' brains to collect key information from stakeholders and the market. This helps members to fully understand the team goals and plans, and what specific actions to take to deliver the target results. As there will likely be changes in the stakeholder needs and market situations, high-performance teams have periodical planning and decision-making systems built in monthly or quarterly where they continuously review the progress, make necessary modifications in the plan to solve problems, or capture new opportunities over a period of 12 months.

Where do you see any improvement or strengthening opportunities in your team's planning and decision-making processes?

2) **Core team process and operating system** - This is about how the team works together while sharing necessary information in the team in a timely manner. It covers the end-to-end core process the team operates. If the team is physically creating something, then the core team process covers planning, ordering materials, processing materials, producing out-

put, and delivering the product to the customer.

Poor performing teams do not have a solid team process or a good information and opinion sharing mechanism in the team. Members with good relationships may share information and work well together to maximize their output, while other members, especially those who do not have a good relationship with other members, are working in a silo, and so they are missing out on the opportunities of collaborating with other members. People cannot act on something they don't know, and the leader cannot assume that all members know the entire team's processes and information sharing mechanisms. This often creates unnecessary and unproductive meetings and frustration in the team.

High-performance teams, on the other hand, have a solid core team process where team members understand the entire core process of the team, where and how they work together, support each other, and collaborate to deliver stronger results. For example, a high-performance computer software sales team I worked with have shared and educated the entire sales process, key activities, key performance indicators, and information throughout the process among its sales members, system engineers, and customer service members. This made the entire team strengthen their collaboration and information sharing, knowing how to work together to best achieve the team goal. As a result, they have significantly reduced their sales cycle as well as customer claims, which has resulted in increased revenue and customer satisfaction.

Any strategic changes in the product and services or target customers or market can impact this core team process. Also, in today's volatile market with advanced information technology, many teams are experiencing vast changes in their processes. For example, a training team who used to offer the training program mostly in a classroom format is now shifting to an online combined with a blended learning format (classroom learning, on-the-job application, and online learning support). So, their entire process has changed from planning to preparing to executing to evaluating to upgrading the learning programs.

Where do you see any improvement or strengthening areas in your team process and information sharing mechanism? Once you identify improvement needs and change the process, it's usually good to put the new process in writing, using a flow chart diagram. Please see an example of work flow chart below.

Work Flow Chart Format Example

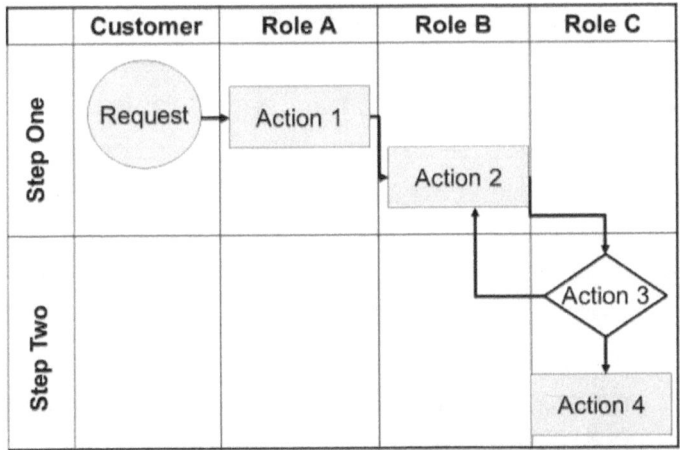

3) **Work process/systems used across members** - This is about improving, modifying or revamping individual processes and systems that go across members

and/or stakeholders, which requires work coordination and collaboration. This intra-team and inter-team process can change when there is a change in the core team process as well as changes in customer requirements.

Also, changes in technology or changes in individual tasks and processes can impact on intra-team processes and systems. For example, waiters' order-taking methods at many restaurants are moving from manual to electronic systems, using iPads; and the order-taking information goes immediately to the kitchen. While this system change improved customer satisfaction, it also created a new workflow, work behaviors, and skills, requiring new training.

2. **Robust people processes and systems** - People processes and systems are keys to ensuring all team members are at their peak no matter where they are in the life cycle of their corporate life.

Teams who don't have sufficient people systems usually suffer from low employee engagement, poor employee development, frequent employee complaints, and high attrition.

High-performance teams have effective team development systems, including recruiting and hiring systems, orientation programs, learning and development programs, and team development systems to continuously develop people.

a) **Hiring/selection system and process** - High-performance teams have a solid recruiting and hiring process and system, using clear and consistent selection criteria, a set of specific interviewing questions and evaluation methods. This is essential for ensuring the quality of members. What disasters will we create if we hire a person who doesn't fit in the role nor the team? If we hire the wrong person, it would be a nightmare for both the team and the hired individuals, as the individual will not be happy or productive, and the entire team will also not feel happy about working with unhappy people, resulting in lowered energy and productivity in the team.

In today's diverse workforce with various cultural backgrounds, the team leader needs to take a systemic approach to recruiting and selecting the best-fit newcomers, involving team members while partnering with HR people when available. Recruitment interviews are important opportunities for the team to give the right first impression to future members, which help both the team and candidates identify the optimal fit with each other. Thus, those who are involved in a hew hire selection process need to understand hiring/selection standards, hiring principles, effective interviewing skills, and hiring steps. Members in great teams understand and are able to execute those fundamentals. Also, as there is a limitation in selecting new hires just by interviewing, some psychometric assessment tools are also used to understand how the candidates' personality, values, and motivation sources may fit with the team and their roles.

However, many team leaders are not equipped with that fundamental knowledge and skills. Many leaders select newcomers based on their preference - communication style and personality matching with their preference and experiences. At the same time, this type of gut feeling selection with unconscious biases cause a rejection of good candidates simply because their first impression did not appeal interviewers. That's why there are so many hiring mistakes, and the median number of years that wage and salary workers had been with their current employer was as low as 4.2 years, as reported by the U.S. Bureau of Labor in January 2016.

When hiring new members, the leader needs to make sure they fit with the desired team culture, not just the existing culture, especially if the team is in a transition phase toward the new vision, strategy or the new culture.

b) **Orientation** - What kind of orientation do you offer to newly hired members? How is that working for the new hires?

Why is orientation important? People are usually very susceptible to make a change in their mindset, behaviors or habits when they enter a new environment. So, this is a great opportunity to help new members modify their thinking and habits to get ready for the new work environment. High-performance teams give a thorough orientation to newcomers to ensure they understand and are aligned with the team's core systems and principles as well as expectations of them.

In addition to the company orientation done by Human Resources, high-performance teams help them understand the team, the team mission, vision, and values, the work the team does, the work systems, key stakeholders, and environment. More importantly, they truly welcome and personally connect with new members, which makes them feel welcomed, engaged, and builds a high hope for working in the team.

Poor teams do not spend much effort on team orientation, and just briefly introduce new members to the team, desk, and work they will do very mechanically. The worst teams do not give any sign of welcome, a sense of appreciation, opportunities for expectation match around the work, including specific accountability, work standards, key operating procedures, and training plans. This type of orientation will certainly turn off new members, and even make them question why they joined this company. Missing out this alignment and engagement opportunity can cost the team a lot later on, such as losing newcomers within 12 months or creating disengaged new members and unproductive teams.

c) **Member development system** - How are your members learning and developing in your team to further enhance their performance and on-the-job effectiveness? How are you measuring their growth and development?

On top of enabling members through giving feedback, coaching and learning, and development opportunities to help achieve their work plans, leaders in high performing teams have a system and process in mind for how to keep developing the members. This system will help leaders to plan and act on members development systemically, not sporadically. It also helps members think, plan, and act on their professional and career growth long-term on their own without being told by leaders or by Human Resource learning and development staff. The member development system also plays an important role in building autonomous and self-directed cultures in the team.

The member development system covers beyond skill development and is integrated with members' career development planning - how members are growing their professional and personal capabilities and building their career in the team. In high performing teams, leaders discuss with members their thinking on their career plans, possible moves inside and outside the team, necessary experiences, a time frame and required competency to get there. Formal member development and career planning is usually done as soon as their work plans are made. As many organizations have mid-year or quarterly progress reviews, this can be done several times in the fiscal year and when there is a change or need for changing the plan.

People Processes

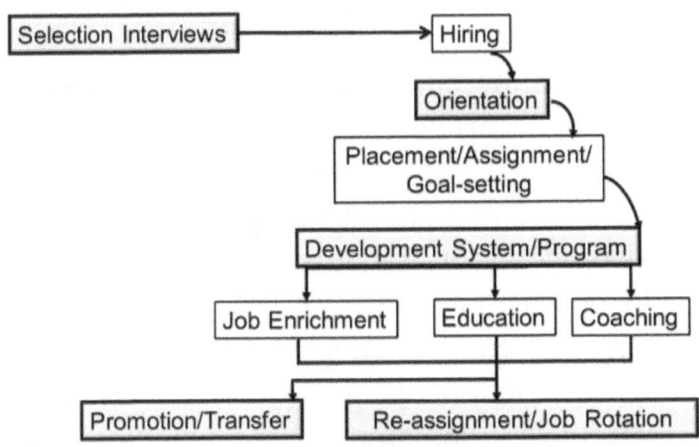

3. **Team development systems/processes** - In contrast to the people development system, the team development system is about building the team capacity and capability to create synergy to attain team goals in a systemic manner. The objective of team development system/process is 2-fold: to (1) build and improve a team structure and system to deliver the goals, and (2) make the team more cohesive. A great team isn't built overnight. It takes a series of phases to become a great team. I've seen many teams who keep using inefficient processes and methods without making any changes. The leaders' important job is to grow the team steadfastly.

This requires a conscious effort by both leaders and members.

The first objective is linked with and directed toward achieving the team mission and vision. Imagine you time traveled 10 years forward from now and just achieved your team mission and vision. What are key driving forces to deliver the strategy? What structure, or key roles and positions, do your team have to achieve your goals? How many members do you have in the team? What new processes and systems do you see that better meet stakeholders' needs and wants? Once you identify improvement opportunities, then you can start developing ways to build the new team process and system, involving your members.

There are many companies who have been accredited in ISO 9000 and 14000 yet experience quality issues and compliance scandals. This problem happens when the team start-up was not thorough and effective – the leader did not conduct a sufficient mutual understanding opportunity to start building relationships. I've seen this happen in the early stage of many mergers and acquisitions, as they are so much concerned about getting the newly integrated organizations up and running. If this is the case, team leaders in the organization needs to re-build their integrated teams later on. The second objective of a team development system is to further accelerate trust among members and build stronger team cultures to improve team performance. Effective team processes and systems are useful when the team has trusting and high performing cultures.

4. **Meeting processes (e.g., problem-solving and decision-making)** – A meeting is one of key improvement opportunities in most organizations to discuss and align. There are many meetings taking place in teams and organizations. I hear a lot of complaints from both managers and members that they attend too many meetings that they take up too much of their time, but they do not add much value to their work. Some meetings have too many attendees who are not actively participating; and some other meetings do not have the key stakeholders to make decisions. Their frustration gets escalated when the meeting doesn't produce an agreed decision

or solution to the issue, which was the objective of the meeting.

High performing teams have a clear meeting process and system that everyone understands and follows - everyone understands the meeting's goals, agenda, their roles, and they fully participate in the meeting to achieve the meeting's goals. Obviously, the participants are fulfilled at the end of the meeting, as they contributed to determining the solution or attaining the meeting's goals. The leader needs to help make the meeting fruitful and efficient, so that members fully utilize their expertise and potential to add value to enhancing team performance - never feeling frustrated and drained.

5. **Productive work environment:** You may have seen various companies and their offices, and probably sensed some sort of team or organization culture once you stepped into the office - some are neatly organized, some others are a bit busy and chaotic. In addition to the way people work and communicate in the workplace, the office layout, walls, desk arrangement, partitions, and how their workspace looks can also indicate the culture and

productivity of the team. How does the office layout and workspace of your team look? How are the office design, layout, and workspace helping members work, communicate, and collaborate productively?

1) Office design, layout and artifacts - Are the office design and layout user-friendly and help members work, communicate, and collaborate effectively? Office design, walls, and layout can project team values and culture. For example, if team values include collaboration and innovation, office design, layout, and color could be open, spacious, and bold, with artifacts projecting a collaborative and innovative image. Or, if there are high partitions to separate members, it can project a "work independently" and "Don't talk in the team" atmosphere.

2) Individual workspace - Can each member concentrate on their task with a feeling professionalism and creativity? Are they distracted by much noise? So, even though the team may be encouraged to collaborate, there needs to be a good mixture of private and collaborative work-

stations. Are their desks and chairs ergonomically designed for members' body and health? Is there natural lighting?

When doing the above actions, I suggest you benchmark the best practices of the related functions of other companies both inside and outside of the industry you are in, so that all the team members expand their horizons and upgrade their standards of excellence. Through benchmarking activities, the team will know and familiarize themselves about key success factors, systems, processes, policies, technologies, and work environments. How should we do benchmarking? There are several ways. One of easiest way is to check the companies listed in the Fortune 500. If you check the website and annual reports of the top 10 companies in the 500, and also the top 3 of your industry, you will be able to learn a lot of useful information, such as what trends those top companies are trying to create in the near future, what challenges they are foreseeing in the marketplace, and what strategy they are working on. You can use that information to develop your team strategy and competitive edges. So, if you are leading IT team, ask the members to check IT savvy companies to learn from them.

See below chart indicating typical characteristics of the team with and without "Enhancing System and Environment."

Characteristics of the team with and without "Enhancing Systems and Environment."

Team Characteristics "with Enabling Systems and Environment"	Team Characteristics "without Enabling Systems and Environment"
• Aligned and cohered team	• Unaligned and fragmented team
• User-friendly process/system	• Complicated process/system
• Thinks holistically/systemically	• Thinks narrowly, focusing on self
• Collaborative operations/culture	• Not working well together
• Timely information sharing	• Lack of information sharing
• Effective decision-making	• Poor decision-making
• Minimal frustration in the team	• Frustrated people are everywhere
• User-friendly lay-	• Stifled work envi-

out/workspace • Able to focus on core work • Highly productive	ronment/space • Lots of distractions at work • Low productivity

Key Principles of Enhancing Systems and Environment

1) **Mission and stakeholder-focused** - Work systems and processes need to be primarily focused on achieving the team mission and customers' needs, and secondarily on members and other stakeholders.

2) **Continuous improvement** - As environments and customer needs are constantly changing, leaders need to continuously look for opportunities for improvement and innovation to achieve the team mission and vision.

3) **Systemic** - One change in the system will influence other systems and subsystems. So, the leader needs to holistically analyze total systems and decide the necessary actions to achieve sustainable en-

hancement of the systems and work environment to be productive.

4) **Data-based** - In order for the team to make optimal decisions, they need to set measures, track the progress, and make adjustments and improvements based on data.

5) **Participative** - The leader needs to promote a participative approach, involving key members and stakeholders to effectively make systemic changes as well as to empower and engage members.

Key Leadership Actions: While there are many areas leaders can take the lead in to make the team system and environment productive in line with the team values, we will introduce five effective, practical, and easy-to-implement actions - "work simplification," "team development workshop," "effective meetings," "Orientation for newcomers," and "workplace enhancement."

1. Work Simplification Workshop - This engaging activity will be effective to simplify the work taking place in the team. All team members are involved in this workshop to identify work improvement opportunities. I have done this once a year right before the annual work planning. Why? Because the output from this work simplification workshop will be put in the members' annual work plan for the next fiscal year. This will be a great opportunity to pick up all the low hanging fruits to improve team productivity. Members get really excited about making their work effective and efficient.

Goals: To identify priority opportunities for improvement for the coming fiscal year and determine who will lead the improvement effort in the team.

Actions: 2-3 hour meeting, involving all team members

Preparation/Materials: The team leader will announce the goal, agenda, and date to the team one month prior to the workshop.

As indicated in the prior section, I also suggest you ask each member to benchmark the best practices of the related functions of other companies both inside and outside of the industry you are in, so that members familiarize themselves about key success factors, systems, processes, policies, technologies, and work environments.

Needed materials are flip-chart (or wall-paper or whiteboard), several stacks of PostIt notes, colored markers.

Flow:

1) **Introduction** (5 min) - The leader announces the objective, goal, and agenda of the workshop.

2) **Icebreaker** (20 min) - Ask each member to imagine their best and worst work day and draw a picture that signifies best and worst day on a flip-chart (5 min); then, ask them to introduce their best and worst day in the team. This fun activity can work to help members visualize what's working and what's not working and help them to think of their ideal work situations and what can be improved.

3) **Brainstorming improvement areas** (20 min) - Introduce the objective and activity of brainstorming and ask the members to brainstorm anywhere they feel improvements are needed. e.g., "Having those best and worst days on your mind, I want you to individually brainstorm any areas

you think we can improve on in our work and put those improvement ideas on PostIt notes - writing one improvement idea on one PostIt note. Your improvement idea could include any work processes, inefficient ways of working, unnecessary activities, or activities taking up too much effort for limited benefit, or inefficient systems and policies. The more ideas, the better. You will have 15 minutes for writing your improvement ideas. So, let's get started."

4) **Sharing improvement ideas** (30 - 40 min) - Introduce three buckets of improvement ideas and ask each member to present their ideas and place the PostIt notes in the categorized buckets (flipchart or wall-paper or whiteboard). 3 categories of improvement ideas are:
   1) **Quick Win** - Can be improved by our team
   2) **Collaboration** - Need another group's collaboration to implement
   3) **High Impact** - Need multi-functional effort to implement: To help members focus their mind, it's good if you collect ideas for one category, then move on-

to the next category, e.g., (1) quick win, (2) collaboration, and (3) high impact. If you have less than 10 members, use the Round Robin method for members to introduce their ideas, i.e., one person introduces one idea, the next person introduces an idea similar to the prior person's idea, and the same goes true for the next person. When all ideas around the initial idea are done, we will move onto the new idea. (This is a good method to hear all the voices and also be able to group similar ideas while collecting them.)

4) **Consolidate Ideas** (15 - 20 min) - Assign members to review, consolidate, and integrate similar ideas to finalize the improvement idea for each category. Ask the assigned members to present the finalized ideas.

5) **Select key ideas and leaders** (15 - 20 min) - First, ask each member to vote for the top 3 effective ideas for each category. Second, summarize voting results of important improvement ideas - top 3 - 5 for each category. Third, tell each member they need

to own one improvement idea, and ask for volunteers for leading those key improvement ideas. Fourth, confirm leaders for improvement ideas, and tell them to think through and report back goals, key actions, and completion timings within a week.

6) **Wrap-up** (5 min) - Appreciate everyone's contributions, confirm next steps, and show high expectation.

2. Team Development Workshop - All teams have some improvement opportunities, and high performing teams are constantly enhancing their capacity and capability. This activity can be done any time, but it is especially effective if done when the team is formed. The team can understand their progress by conducting a team development workshop once a year.

Goals: To identify strengths, weaknesses, and improvement areas of the current team and determine action plans.

Actions: 2-3 hour meeting, involving all team members

Preparation/Materials: The team leader will announce the goal, agenda, and date to the team one month prior to the workshop. The team leader then sends out the survey on team effectiveness. (Please see survey example on the following page.)

Needed materials at the workshop are flip-chart (or wall-paper or whiteboard), several stacks of PostIt notes, colored markers.

Flow:

1) **Introduction** (5 min) - The leader announces the objective, goal, and agenda of the workshop.

2) **Icebreaker** (20 min) - First, ask each member to recall the best team they have experienced to date and identify its working factors (3 min). Second, ask the team to share their experience of the great team and their key strengths or working factors, and then decide key success factors of that team (15 min). Fourth, ask them to report back their key success factor list (2 - 5 min). This activity will help members remember and align the overall working factors and framework of effective teams.

3) **introduce team effectiveness model** (15 min) - Linking with the output of an icebreaker, the leader introduces and explains six elements of effective teams, i.e., (1) aligned direction, (2) leadership at the top and ownership of each member, (3) clear roles and responsibilities, (4) effective work systems, (5) open communication, and (6) trusting relationships. Second, ask each member to think and identify the team's strong areas and improvement areas.

4) **Review team survey results** (30 - 40 min) - The leader shares the team effectiveness survey results - the rating for each element, and then asks the members to identify and share the strengths of the team and how those strengths are working (15-20 min). Next, ask members to think and share key improvement areas and why they think they are key (15-20 min).

5) **Discuss and identify team development plans** (30 - 40 min) - First, ask each member to identify and write on PostIt notes action plans to further leverage the

team's strengths to increase its performance - one idea on one PostIt note (7 - 10 min). Second, share, discuss, and determine the top 3 action ideas to implement (7 - 10 min). Third, ask the team to identify and write action plans to improve team performance - one improvement idea on one PostIt note (7 - 10 min). Fourth, ask members to share, discuss, and determine the top 3 action ideas to implement (7 - 10 min). Fifth, summarize key action ideas and ask for volunteers to lead each action idea. Lastly, confirm leaders for each plan and ask them to report back goals, key actions, and completion timings within a week.

6) **Wrap-up** (5 min) - Appreciate everyone's contributions, confirm next steps, and show high expectation.

3. Effective Meeting - Many teams see improvement opportunities during their team meetings, and the leader is in the best position to improve meeting efficiency. Of course, the leader can ask the team for their perspectives and improvement points from their current team meeting, so that the whole team understand and align together on improving current meeting procedure. But, if you have already found the improvement areas, you can just implement better meeting protocol.

Goals: To be able to achieve the meeting objective as scheduled, more efficiently, and energizing all the participants.

Actions: The leader will plan and implement more effective meetings, engaging all participants. There are three phases in effective meetings. The team leader will announce the objective for improved team meeting protocol, merit of change, and key changes in procedure and roles of the members one month prior to the next meeting.

One of good examples of meeting agenda is called an "Action Agenda" which indicates the project name, meeting objectives and expected outcomes, required pre-work for members, participating members and specific discussion topics with goals, who leads the discussion and how, and expected outcomes from the topic. (See an example on the following page.)

1) **Preparation phase:** The team leader will ensure all the members understand the goal and agenda (action agenda) of the meeting, participants roles, and the date 2 - 3 weeks prior to the meeting. Make sure the following items are available at the meeting venue:
   - Flip-chart (or wall-paper or whiteboard), PostIt notes, and markers
   - A clock

2) **Meeting Phase - Meeting protocol:**

   (1) **Opening:** The leader/meeting chairperson will thank members for joining the meeting in time and make an opening remark. You need to start on time as planned.

   (2) **Check-in:** This is a brief warm-up for getting all members ready to participate in the meeting as well as connecting them emotionally. A check-in topic/question is something positive members experienced recently or will experience soon, such as, "What was a recent success (Win)?" "What change have your made recently (Change)?" "What did you recently learn (Learn)?"

"What fun did you had over the weekend (Fun)?" Check-in questions also include members' perspective or thoughts around the subject related to the meeting theme, for example, if the meeting theme is innovation, you may ask "What was the best or wildest innovation you ever experienced?" Also, if it is the kick-off meeting where participants don't know each other, then, a self-introduction with a personal flavor will be a good check-in. The leader will introduce check-in topic and ask each member to share their answers; (30 second to 1 minute per member).

(3) **Meeting Introduction:** Introduce the overall meeting objectives, expected outcomes, agenda, allotted time, and responsible person for each agenda topic, ground rule, logistics and end time. Ask for questions and clarifications.

Ground rules: If the team doesn't have meeting ground rules, the team leader can lead the discussion to co-create them for the team. e.g., *"As we would* *like to make this meeting as productive and collaborative as possible, let's create some ground rules for running it for our team. Please think individually of several effective actions desirable in a productive and collaborative meeting among a truly high-performance team and identify the top 5 desired behaviors. You have 60 seconds." After one minute, "Thank you, and in 5 minutes, please share your thoughts and determine our desired meeting behaviors, up to 7, as our meeting ground rules."*

Logistics may include:
- Start time, breaks (if needed), and end time.
- Topic owners will lead the discussion and summarize the conclusions and indicated actions.
- There will be specific conclusions and next steps at the end of each discussion topic.
- Parking lot - If any comments or questions outside of the scope of today's topic are raised during the discussion, I will put those on this flip-chart, which we call a "Parking

Lot," so that we won't forget, and then we will come back to them after this meeting or on a later date.

(4) **Discussions:** Start the discussion on the first topic. The leader or owner of the topic will introduce a specific objective, expected outcomes, and how to proceed and conclude the discussion. The key background of the topic may be shared so that everyone is on the same page.

There are several discussion methods or procedures as follows:
- **Free discussion** - participants freely share their thoughts and ideas with little intervention by the chairperson. This is time a consuming, inefficient method if the members are not used to discussing logically and constructively.
- **Itemized discussion** where a chairperson asks structured, itemized questions, such as, (1) current issues, (2) root causes, (3) solution ideas, (4) benefits and potentials from the identified solu-

tions, (5) possible risks and watch-out for each solution idea, (6) evaluate solutions, (7) finalize solution and responsible person(s). This approach will help participants attention and thoughts focus on itemized the topic and keep them from derailing discussions.

- **Brainstorming** - Instead of asking members to share their thoughts and ideas verbally, a chairperson introduce a brainstorming method, key principles, and ask for contributions. I recommend you use brainstorming by writing on PostIt notes, as introduced several times on this book, as it is time efficient and helps collect everyone's ideas and thoughts in a limited time. This is in contrast to a typical verbal brainstorming or discussion where a handful of vocal people dominate the discussion taking too much time without getting ideas from the rest of the members.

At the end of each topic, make sure there is a clear conclusion and specific next steps with identified responsible persons and a target completion date/timing. The discussion leader/chairperson is responsible for taking notes on key discussions, conclusions, and next steps (indicated actions and responsible persons).

When there are comments or questions raised out of the scope of the topic, the leader will write those comments and questions on the "Parking Lot" (Flipchart).

(5) **Meeting wrap-up:** Ask each topic leader/owner to briefly summarize key outcomes and specific next steps along with completion timing. Thank topic owner's leadership, appreciate everyone's contributions in making the meeting highly productive, and state your high expectations on the follow-up actions and completion.

3) **Follow-up -** This is the responsibility of topic owners and assigned responsible persons for each action item. You may not need to officially follow-up, but you

may ask topic owners and action leaders about their progress in an informal way.

If you have a team intranet, you may include space for meeting summaries and progress of indicated actions so that all members understand the status of each discussion item and indicated actions.

Action Agenda Format

Project :			
Date/Time :		Location :	
Objective :			
Expected Outcomes :			
Pre-work :			
Members :			

Time:	Topics & Objectives	Who / How	Expected Outcomes

4. Orientation and induction program - This is in addition to the orientation program conducted by the H R department. If done well, new members will feel engaged, energized, and be further committed to do a good job in the team. The leaders and other members need to be fully excited about welcoming newcomers to the team.

Especially, if you are hiring Millennial, you need to understand and consider their characteristics when developing their orientation program, while we should certainly not generalize and label them into a certain persona. For example, many Millennials value relationships and prefer to get connected and collaborate; they appreciate recognition and feedback, and they are tech-savvy and multi-tasking.

Goals: To make newcomers feel truly welcomed, understood, engaged, and committed to working in the team; also, help them understand the team mission, vision, values, core work, and key stakeholders of the team, key performance index, roles, and responsibilities of newcomers, and the high expectations of them.

Actions: The team will collaborate to conduct an orientation for newcomers. The team leader may ask for a volunteer who wants to lead this work.

1) **Planning phase:** The team will discuss and determine how to make the orientation engaging, exciting, and enabling.

    (1) The assigned project leader will state the objective, goals, and agenda for developing orientation for newcomers.

    (2) Discuss or brainstorm ideas to make the new member orientation truly engaging, energizing, and enabling. Brainstorming using PostIt notes is recommended to identify as many interesting and exciting ideas as possible in just a short 10 - 15 minutes.

    (3) Share their ideas and put them in several categories, such as welcome decoration in the office, welcome kit, welcome lunch or get-together, mutual understanding event, learning materials, induction program, office tour to understand the team stakeholders, so on and so forth.

(4) Determine key orientation ideas. Ask members to review all the ideas and vote for ones that will make the orientation the most engaging, energizing, and enabling for the new members.

(5) Finalize the plan and responsibility of each member to implement the plan.

(6) Prepare all the materials and execute as planned, including putting welcome decoration in the team space and on the desk of a new member.

2) **Implementation Phase:**

(1) Welcome new members into the team workplace, showing excitement and appreciation for joining the team.

(2) Offer mutual understanding sessions (rather than immediately introducing and explaining the team and work). Remember Millennials value relationship and connectedness.

(3) Implement the rest of the orientation as planned. Keep the session as interactive and engaging as possible. Please make it action-oriented, as human be-

ings learn best through experience. Do not give boring one-way presentations, which will put the participants asleep. Offer welcome a lunch or get-together early in the program.

(4) Interview newcomers to learn their takeaways and feedback to the program, as well as inviting their questions and confirmation about the team and their roles. In so doing, help them visualize their personal vision, which is in line with "autonomy and self-directedness" of the team culture.

Based on newcomers' feedback, make any changes and modifications to the future orientation plans if needed.

Indicate to new members their future learning and development plans with possible timing.

Also, appreciate all the team and celebrate the collaboration and successful completion of welcoming new members.

3) **Follow-up phase -** A few weeks following the orientation, interview new members to

understand their status, progress, and any questions and concerns about their work, respond to their questions and concerns and give coaching as appropriate.

Offer additional or planned training and learning programs at an appropriate time. After completion of each program, please be sure to get new members' takeaway and indicated actions. Also, follow-up on their reapplication of their newly learned skills and knowledge on their job to help enhance their performance. Remember Millennials value feedback and recognition.

Based on newcomers' feedback, make any changes to the future training and learning programs.

5. Work Environment Enhancement - The objective of this activity is to make the team workspace productive and inspiring in line with the team vision and values.

Goals: To make the team workspace user-friendly, so that members can work effectively, collaboratively, and feeling energized while working. The team workspace projects the image of the team vision and values.

Actions: The team will collaborate to improve the team workspace to be productive, energizing, and user-friendly. The team leader will ask for a volunteer to lead this work. There are three phases in this activity - planning phase, action phase, and consolidation phase.

1) **Planning phase:** The team will discuss and determine how to make the team workspace more productive and energizing.

    (1) The assigned project leader will state the objective, goals, and overall approach for enhancing the team workspace.

    (2) Discuss or brainstorm ideas to make the workplace productive and energizing. Brainstorming using PostIt notes is recommended to identify as many interesting and exciting ideas as possible in just a short 10 - 15 minutes.

    (3) Share their ideas and put them in several categories, such as office layout, colors, individual workspace, collaboration area, policy, artifacts, so on and so forth.

(4) Determine key work environment enhancement ideas. Ask members to review all the ideas and vote for ones that will make the workplace productive, energizing, and in line with the team vision and values.

(5) Finalize the plan and responsibility of each member to implement the plan.

2) **Implementation Phase:**

(1) Execute as planned.

(2) Review the outcome

(3) Appreciate and celebrate the collaboration and successful completion.

3) **Follow-up and consolidation phase -** A few weeks after the completion, collect feedback from each member to ensure everything is working as planned and expected. Do any changes if needed to make the team workspace and environment productive and energizing.

In Summary

Team systems, processes, and work environment will shape members' attitudes and behaviors and help build the team culture. High performing teams are intentionally designed to systemically deliver great results. Leaders are responsible for building high performing systems, processes, environments, and cultures. Leaders' enhancing actions include (1) team processes and systems improvement and innovation, (2) people and team development systems, (3) meeting effectiveness enhancement, (4) work environments and artifacts strengthening, and (5) a high-performance culture development, involving all in the team.

One of effective ways to building high-performance systems and processes is benchmarking, involving all the team members. Both the leader and members search current best practices inside and outside of the industry and identify what those great teams are doing differently than the rest. You will certainly find lots of improvement opportunities from them, which you can apply in the team. Benchmarking can also help the team get motivated about stepping up to the next level.

Another important practice is to conduct a customer and a team survey to learn the current strengths and improvement areas. As you cannot do too many things at a time, the leader should help the team identify the top 3 – 5 areas to improve or innovate and focus the team's efforts on those top priority areas. Please note that many failing teams often do too many things at a time and cannot complete those tasks excellently due to time and resource constraints.

System Effectiveness Check List

	Key Items	OK	NG
Robust Work Systems	• Core team processes • Customer interfacing processes • Meeting process • Information sharing systems • User-friendly technologies • Work policies		
Enabling People & Team Systems	• Hiring processes • Orientation • People development systems • Team development systems • Promotion policy • Transfer policy		
Energizing & Professional Work Environment	• Office layout • Office design/colors • Desk arrangement • Artifacts		

Please check below chart to see how you are constantly helping the team to create a high preforming culture and capability.

Dos and Don'ts of Leaders when Enabling

Dos	Don'ts
• Think long-term mission/vision • Think strategically • Focus on external customers • Continually benchmark • Role model systemic changes • Help members understand the team success factors/framework • Encourage members to be systemic thinkers • Create a churn of continually improving and innovating • Focus on building strong cultures • Balance business and people systems	• Think mostly about a fiscal year • Focus on tasks, plans, and events. • Spend energy on internal politics • Mostly care about competitors • Focus on parts, not on systems • Don't teach members in team framework and success factors • Don't give feedback or coaching on systemic thinking • Keep using the same systems, processes, and environments • Don't influence cultures • Mostly focus on business and don't build people/team systems

Chapter 9

Putting It All Together

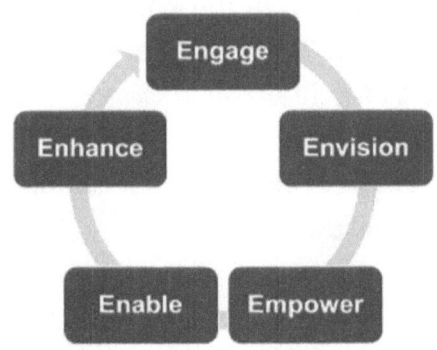

Linking 5 key leadership actions with workplace problems

As shared in Chapter 1, problems at the workplace in many parts of the world are stress and disengaged members, which negatively affect productivity and health of teams. Some of the reasons for these problems are a lack of meaning in work, poor relationships with colleagues, work stress from being pushed to do more with less, work environments that are not user-friendly, and worse, bullying and a wide variety of harassment.

Maslow's needs hierarchy applies to both private and work life. We want to lead our life healthily, respectfully, and productively as a human. At the workplace, people need not only physical and psychological safety but also good human relationships, a sense of growth, autonomy, and meaningful work to feel and experience self-worth and self-actualization. Work doesn't have to be just a means to live. People look for a workplace where they can work happily, collaboratively, and productively.

In order to solve many of the current problems members are suffering from, leaders need to ensure the following in our workplace:

1. "Meaning in work" that lights the hearts of members

2. "Autonomy and self-directedness" that motivates members to be creative and confident

3. "Growth and mastery" that encourages members to move forward

4. "Psychological safety" that heals and opens up the hearts of members

5. "A stress-free and productive work environment" that helps members to work healthily, efficiently, and productively

Who is in the best position to create the above elements in the workplace?

Yes, it's the leaders - supervisors, team leaders, managers or executives, regardless of their title. Leaders' five key actions are the following:

1. "Engage" to help build psychological safety, trust, and community in the team.

2. "Envision" to create meaning, and inspire members by co-creating a mission, vision, values, and strategic focus for the team.

3. "Empower" to help members to be self-directed by having them develop and implement team plans.

4. "Enable" to assist members to grow and master professional and personal competency.

5. "Enhance environment and systems" to build a productive, collaborative, and energetic workplace and culture.

Key team effectiveness factors are (a) inspiring direction, (b) effective leadership, (c) clearly defined roles, (d) robust working environment and systems, (e) open and effective communication, and (f) trusting relationships. For the team to collaborate in a productive way, the leader needs to build those key team effectiveness elements.

Relationship between Problems and Leadership Actions in the Team

Problems	Needs	5 Leaders' Actions
• Disengaged employees • Poor relationship • Bullying/harassment • Lack of cooperation • Stressed members • High turnover • Decreased productivity • Decreased business	• More meaningful work • More autonomy and self-directedness • Growth and mastery • Good relationships • Psychological safety • More innovation • More cooperative and productive work system	• Envision to create meaning • Empower members to execute team plans more autonomously • Enable members to grow mastery • Engage members to build trust • Enhance work system and environment

There are no fixed methods or order to implement those five leaders' actions. Leaders need to know when and how to practice those actions to further enhance team performance and health. Which actions to focus on depends on where your team is right now in their development phases as well as your team's strengthening and improvement areas.

The Four Phases of Team Development

Before discussing how to orchestrate the five leaders' actions, I want to briefly touch upon four phases of team development all teams go through. Once you understand the model and where your team is, you will be able to see more clearly what actions you need to focus on right now.

Bruce Tuckman (1965) studied various teams and identified four phases teams go through to grow and perform.

1. **"Forming" phase**

    This is when a team is formed, and members start working together for the first time. The team discusses and builds some structures by deciding goals, roles, and plans. There are differences between members in terms of experience, competency, and maturity levels. In this phase, members tend to work rather independently, as they don't know each other well, and the trust level is still not high. Some members might be reserved and careful so as not to make mistakes or step on other's toes.

2. **"Storming"**

As time goes on, members start experiencing some discrepancy between their initial expectation and the reality in the team, such as work standards and work quality, encountering unexpected problems, experiencing personality clash with other members, or working on something different than what's written on their job description. Some members voice their opinions to the leader and colleagues. This is the phase where the team encounters several expectation mismatches, feels stress and anxiety, and the trust level in the team goes down. The team needs to identify how to understand and collaborate with each other to achieve the team goals. In the worst case, teams stay in this stage for a long time and eventually collapse.

3. **"Norming"**

As members have learned to communicate with each other, work together better, and solved some team issues, they work on (re-)aligning roles and work standards, establishing better policy and rules, coordinating work, and enhancing work processes and systems. This is the phase the team is more aligned on goals, roles, and how to communicate, coordinate, and collaborate with each other. The trust level in the team increases as they move the project forward. Also, members tend to enhance their professional and personal skills to increase their performance and achieve team goals. Some members willingly take on leadership in the absence of the leader.

4. **"Performing"**

As members are aligned and learn to coordinate and collaborate as a team and improve their trust and competency levels, the team is now able to achieve their goals consistently. All members possess solid ownership and expertise in their role as well as a strong communication ability. As they collaborate well to create synergism in the team, they often deliver exceptional results. However, as the market environment, customers, competitors, or technologies change constantly, if the team doesn't keep up with those changes, it will slip down to the norming or storming phase. A change of leaders and members can also cause the team to go down to the storming or norming phase, as it can often change team dynamics.

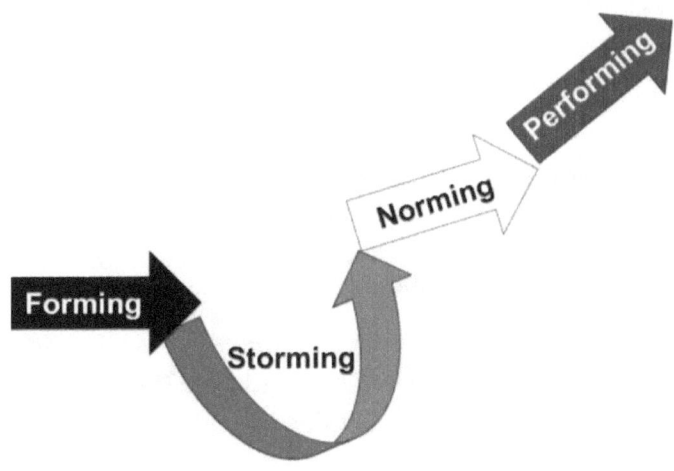

Key Characteristics of Four Team Development Phases

Forming	Storming	Norming	Performing
• *Forming of the team with hopes & fear* • Hopes • Understand objectives • Curiosity and learning • Lack of cohesiveness • Varied quality and competency • Some reservation of fear of failure	• *Problems showing up and trust going down* • Some members speaking up and complaining • Some members staying outside • Increasing bias toward other members • Lowered motivation and trust in the team	• *Building capability and systems* • Aligning work process, norms, system, etc. • Adjusting behaviors to situations/other members styles • Increased trust and coordination • Increased capability • Increased morale in the team	• *Collaborating for great results* • Functioning as an aligned self-directed team • Strong ownership of from all members • Fully capable of delivering great results • Strong trust and collaboration to create synergy

THE SECRET OF HIGH IMPACT LEADERS

Know where your current team is on this development paths

Of the above four phases, which phase is your team now in? Why or what symptoms do you see to say your team is in that phase?

Knowing where your team is, how do you want to implement "envision," "empower," "enable," "engage," and "enhance" in your team's development? Which actions are more important or a higher priority than others?

Which Phase?	Why/What symptoms?	Your Indicated Actions?

Hints for Understanding Your Priority of Your Team Development

1) The top priority of the forming phase is aligning the team direction (what, why, and how) and building relationship.

2) High-performance teams have built all the six key team effectiveness factors early, even at the forming stage. So they may experience a short and shallow storming phase.

3) Most teams experience the "Storming" phase; and those who poorly executed "Forming" will experience a longer and more chaotic "Storming" phase.

4) Proactive problem-solving involving members during the "Storming" phase usually makes the team stronger when done well.

5) The leader needs to navigate the team to continuously improve and innovate throughout the development phase, so as not to slip down.

Basic Approach to Strengthening Current Team

While there is no panacea to cure the problems and maximize team performance, I will introduce you to a fundamental approach that can be applied in many team situations. My recommended team development approach is consistent with the way we build the business - strategic planning and implementation process. Just like organization development, which starts from business strategy, team development is best done when it's based on business needs and focused on building team performance and competency in a balanced manner. Its basic steps are:

1) **Assess** (assessment of the situation)

2) **Engage and Envision** (alignment toward a common mission, vision, and values)

3) **Empower** (determine key plans and roles, and implement the plans)

4) **Enhance systems and enable the team** (build productive work systems and environment and equip the team with the

needed competency to run the new systems)

5) **Track the progress and consolidate the plans and system** (build the capability of the members and the team)

Step 1 – Assess: to fully understand current team situations

Why do we need to audit our team?

How often do you take a physical check? Once a year or once every few years? We take some sort of health check to identify illness and symptoms of possible disease so that we can take remedial actions in case there is a need to cure part of our body. Organizations and teams are just like a human body, as they are made up of various parts that are interrelated and interacting with one another to function and produce expected outcomes (or to survive and thrive). Some parts may be functioning great, and some other parts may not be functioning as good as we would hope. We may not be able to know from the surface how well our teams are without conducting a health check, like a human body.

How often do you take a health check of your team? I have asked this question to thousands of managers in the past. And, their response is almost always "Never" with a few exceptions of knowing their team performance and engagement levels through a breakdown of their corporate employee survey. One of key principles in Total Quality Management is "What gets measured gets done." So, if we don't measure to understand the status and progress, people don't pay attention to that thing, and that thing will not be achieved. Maybe that's why employee engagement level is not so high globally.

There are many types of employee surveys, such as satisfaction surveys, engagement surveys, and more complete and detailed organization diagnostics, such as the Malcom Baldrige organization assessment. What we see is what we look for. So, if we want to understand the health of our team, we need to look at our team from a holistic point of view, like our health examination, so that we can diagnose teams' health status systemically. Knowing the data will help us take the right actions to solve current problems or prevent any bad things from happening in the future.

What should we learn through a team assessment? The assessment needs to work as a preventative measure. It's not just a level of member engagement or satisfaction, which is a symptom and doesn't tell us the reason for that symptom. As we already know from Chapter 2, we need to assess and understand what elements or parts of the team are working and not working, which indicates the root cause(s) of our symptoms and health status of the team. So, we should learn about ourselves in terms of our effectiveness of our direction (mission, vision, values, and strategy), leadership, work environment, and systems (structure, decision-making and work processes, information system, people systems), communication effectiveness, and trusting relationships in the team or among the members.

Like a health check of the human body, if we know the problem area and its root cause, we can identify how to cure or improve the current status to achieve a better performance. As in problem-solving techniques, key steps to effective solving of the problem is to identify its root cause, and then identify how to eliminate the root cause from the system. So, we need to assess the team from a holistic perspective;

looking into all team effectiveness elements to understand how good they are and how those elements are interacting and influencing each other to deliver results we want to achieve. So, how are you assessing your team effectiveness now? If not done yet, how are you going to assess it to enhance your team health and performance?

Key dimensions I recommend using for team assessments are consistent with the model introduced in the Chapter 2. It includes six team effectiveness factors plus key outcomes from those factors:

1) **Direction** - clear and inspiring mission, vision and values, and key team strategy

2) **Leadership and membership** - effectiveness of the team leader and ownership and competency of members

3) **Roles** - role clarity and effective division of roles

4) **Systems** - core team process, key work processes, information sharing system, people systems, meeting effectiveness,

customer orientation, improvement and innovations process

5) **Communication effectiveness**

6) **Trusting relationships** among the members

7) **Team culture, member engagement, and team performance** - outcomes of how team effectiveness factors are.

Key steps in assessing team effectiveness and customer satisfaction level

This can be done just a few weeks before the second step of envisioning and engaging. Basic steps for assessing the current team status are to (1) align on the intent of conducting the team survey, (2) develop and determine a survey questionnaire and specific questions for the survey, (3) implement the survey, and (4) collect the survey results and produce the survey report.

- **Alignment of intent and plan** – The first step is alignment among the team members as to why as we are making an effort to enhance team capability, and how we are going about it, starting with running a team survey. We can never skimp this step, as members' buy-in is crucial to making a success of any change effort. If we want to create an engaging, collaborative, and productive culture, we need to be transparent from the beginning of the change effort. We need to lead by example, and role model the desired culture and behaviors from the outset.

- **Developing survey questionnaire** - While you might already have a basic idea about the team survey, customer survey, and key probing areas, please review whether it covers all the key elements of the team or team effectiveness, not just about the team performance and member engagement. A customer survey is about the level of satisfaction of the team services and products for each customer, and how the team is responding to the needs and problems of the customers.

An effective survey not only identifies problems or problematic symptoms, but also their root causes, which will help us identify the right solution to eliminate the problem. Also, we need to make an effort to determine specific and easy-to-understand survey questions, so that members, regardless of their tenure, understand the meaning of questions clearly and easily. The value of the survey depends on both the holisticness of its probing areas and the clarity of survey questions. If both are not met, the survey results are not useful or reliable.

- **Implementation of the survey** - We need to select an implementation timing when members and customers are not super busy during a peak business period or when many members are on business trips or on vacation. We should also avoid the period when there are some special events that can affect members and customers' emotional states, such as before personnel appraisal season or right after an annual evaluation, or a big company ceremony.

- **Produce report** - We collect the survey results and produce the survey report. The key to effective analysis is to identify the correlation between key organizational elements, which we probed, and employee engagement. and then identify key influencing factors or root cause of the problem. The produced report needs to be reviewed by management team, so that they can jointly determine the focus of improvement opportunity, and then, announce to the organization. As this will likely overlap the next step, I will talk more about this in the next section.

- At this point, there is no need to fully analyze the team survey results, as this will be done involving all team members later. However, the survey report can illustrate where the team has strengths and where we may need improvements, and make you feel more comfortable about leading and navigating the team development.

Key Principles:

- *What gets measured gets done!*
- *Identifying a root cause of the problem is an effective way to solve issues!*

Step 2 – Engage and Envision: to build relationships and alignment toward a common mission, vision, and values

As already introduced, envisioning is about creating a desired future state, including the mission, vision, and values of the team - a long-term direction of the team. Engaging is about creating a trusting relationship and community in the team. Member engagement is a never-ending journey, but especially important in the forming stage. How much and what engaging activity is required depends on the level of trust in the team.

Envisioning and engaging is key to the success of team development and change, as one of the key barriers to development and change effort is a lack of commitment and alignment among leaders and key stakeholders along with an unclear direction, as suggested by a series of studies (Larson & LaFasto, 2001). I have personally seen so many teams where the lack of leadership role model and unclear desired future vision have caused poor employee engagement. A member's motivation is affected by an inspiring vision, which creates meaning and purpose for growth and change. To further enhance members' motivation, the leader needs to engage and involve members in creating its vision. If we don't get members involved in this important step, they may not take ownership to execute the plan for achieving the future vision, as they may feel that it's somebody else's idea, not their own. If we do this step right, half of our job is done to significantly improve team culture and performance.

$$C = M \times V \times P \times A$$

If there is a solid trust in the team, you can jump right into envisioning, involving the team, while building on and enhancing a trusting relationship on the way. If your team is relatively new or having some concerns about relationships, you will need to start from engaging, e.g., enhancing mutual understanding and building a relationship and trust, before creating the team direction.

Assuming you need to first build or strengthen the relationships of the team, basic actions to take in this phase are 1) getting members on board and alignment, 2) building and enhancing relationships, and 3) co-creating team direction, e.g., team mission, vision, values, and key focal areas.

- **Getting members on board and alignment** - While the team is already aware of the team development as communicated and aligned before conducting the team assessment, the leader needs to remind the team by introducing a business case for the team development effort to reiterate the importance of it. This is a crucial step to ensure all the members are on board and motivated to collaborate and take on this journey. So, link the story of the change and business case with external environment and stakeholders.

Another key to the success of this leadership message is exhibiting a leader's strong commitment and hope for the enhanced team state passionately and authentically. Ideally, you should have started and practiced new, different mindset, attitudes, language, and behaviors before this date, so members feel the leader is committed to this journey and something new will be certainly taking place.

Also, make your communication 2-way and a dialog, not a monologue. Ask questions to gain member's perspectives, opinions, and concerns. During and after your presentation, leaders need to confirm members' willingness and commitment to get on this team development journey together.

- **Building and enhancing relationship -** Before working on developing an ideal future state of the team, the leader needs to build and enhance relationships and trust in the team. Great collaboration is built on a great relationship in the team. So, help members to get to know each other at a deeper level, and connect with them on an emotional level, which will create a psychologically safe environment and help the team to fully communicate and actively listen to each other.

For enhancing mutual understanding and building relationships at a deeper level, do some of the activities introduced in Chapter 5 "Engage." For example:

- "Pictorial life stories" as self-introduction, followed by Q&As or quizzes on the following day, or

- Self-introduction, sharing (a) where born, (b) my hobby, (c) my most exciting experience to date, (d) why they joined this company/organization

- "My four secrets," sharing four things about yourself or experiences other members may not know, including one lie. This is a fun quiz type self-introduction, where the audience needs to identify which episode was a lie. During self-introduction, everyone records their answers on a PostIt note. After everyone has finished, each member will tell which one was a lie. Those who get most correct guesses will get a prize. This is good for the team or group who have worked together for a long period. Even then, it's difficult to identify the lies of their colleagues.

Either before or after enhancing mutual understanding and building a stronger relationship, it's always good to create "ground rules of the day." The leader asks the team to develop and agree on 5 to 7 ground rules for the day that are important behaviors for everyone to exhibit. For example,

"As we would like to make today's session truly great and fruitful for all of us, I want you to develop and agree on 5 to 7 ground rules for this session. First, let's please spend 1 minute to identify 3 to 5 important behaviors we want from all of us here to exhibit while collaborating today... (one minute.) Now, please work together to share and agree on the most important behaviors to make our session the most meaningful and productive. Please write those ground rules on a flip-chart. Also, please write in a verb form, not a noun."

As you can imagine, team engagement is a never-ending journey. The leader needs to continuously provide the opportunities for the team to expand mutual understanding and build stronger relationships, such as conducting a series of self-introduction, self-disclosure, and self-reflection among the team with various tools and methodologies or running a multi-feedback or 360-degree survey where each team member gives candid feedback to the rest of the team members.

Importantly, at the end of any learning and development session, please give participants opportunity to reflect on the event to identify their new insights and action plans, and then, all members will present their takeaways and indicated actions to build trust and to enhance team performance as well as personal effectiveness. This is the key for team learning as well as for the entire team to learn and reapply the learned skills in real world.

- **Co-creating team direction,** e.g., team mission, vision, values, and key focal area. This is to co-create and align on the team mission, vision, values, and/or culture, so that all members are clear about where we are going, why, and how. This is the very key to creating the meaning of working together for the team - may be the first step to have members engaged in the team and their work.

Team Mission - Some teams develop just a vision, or an ideal future state, but it's always good to start with a team mission or purpose - our reason for being or why we exist in this organization, as it will clarify business reasons for team development. This is something that is connecting all team members and moving forward toward an ideal future together.

Of course, if your team already has its mission statement, you may review the mission statement together to fully align on the purpose of the team. However, instead of telling or showing the existing team purpose or mission, ask the team, *"What is the purpose of this team?"* Then, you record the responses of the team. If they responded correctly, then, ask further how we are currently meeting our mission, and have some discussion around that.

Team Vision. Next, after making sure that all the team members understood and are aligned on the team purpose, you may move on to developing the team vision. Please make no mistake - it's not so much about creating a beautiful statement to write on a plaque to put up on the wall of the room. The key here is to create further excitement around moving toward a future vision. The more inspiring the team mission and vision is, the more engaging and motivated the team become. You may use the **"Cover Story"** activity to co-create the team vision, which is fun and exciting, involving every member (see Chapter 4).

Team Goal. Once the team vision is developed and agreed in the above step, you may discuss and set the mid-term or long-term goals, translating the vision into quantifiable targets or key performance indicators, such as business outcomes, customer satisfaction score, retention, new growth, productivity, profitability, and team engagement score.

Team Values or Culture. Fourth, after aligning on the team mission and/or vision, the leader will help the team co-create the team values or culture. Here, we are defining team values and/or culture. The team value is the base for how the team will be working together to achieve our mission and vision. It will be the guiding values for its members to judge and decide their course of action when encountering a fork in the road. This is another area many teams skimp or skip, which will create chaotic coordination later. I have seen "integrity," "customer-focus," "collaboration," and "innovation" as part of values for high-performance teams. While values are often expressed in a noun form, team culture is often expressed as a verb or in a sentence.

Step 3 – Empower: To empower members to determine key plans and roles to achieve team mission and vision, and then implement those plans.

After finalizing the team mission, vision, and values, the natural next step is to develop and align specific plans to achieve the team direction. So, this step can be done back-to-back with the envisioning and engaging step. Many teams I have supported have done "Engaging," "Envisioning," and the planning portion of "Empowering" during the kick-off meeting, spending 2 days - Day1 for engaging and envisioning, and Day2 for empowering up to strategic planning.

The outcomes of Empowering (planning) are (a) road map toward the vision and (b) goals and key initiatives for this year. The ideal future state and the current state of the team can be filled in right after finalizing the team vision. The roadmap indicates key strategic events (plans) and milestones to reach the ideal team vision, as introduced in the empowerment Chapter.

Example of "Road Map"

Current State (20XX)	Road Map	Ideal Future State (20XX)
• Business results • Customer satisfaction • Customer retention • New growth • Productivity • Profitability • Team effectiveness score • Turnover		• Business results • Customer satisfaction • Customer retention • New growth • Productivity • Profitability • Team effectiveness score • Turnover
Future Trends/Events (+/-): Macro environment Market Customer		

There are five activities the team can do in the planning portion of "Empowering." They are (1) environmental trend search, (2) creating road map, (3) determining short-term goals, (4) reviewing the current status and opportunity, and (5) determining team development plan(s).

1) **Environmental trend search:**

This is for the team to review current environmental trends and then speculate future changes in the environment they may encounter on the way to achieving the team mission and vision. This will be a good exercise to expand the perspectives of the members as well as to align members' assumptions and the opportunities on the environment, market, and customers before creating the road map to long-term goals. In addition to trends, key events in the market relevant to the team or the company could be included, e.g., the Olympics.

Some teams do this methodically and elaborately with lots of preparation by each member beforehand, asking them to study and bring data and information on market, competitors, customers, laws and regulations, technologies, and socio-demographics. Some of them even include the perspectives from the futurists. During the session, they work together to summarize possible future trends on flip charts by category or item. Then, they go over the future trends, discuss and agree on important trends that can impact the team's performance in a negative and positive manner.

Some other teams choose to do this simply and impromptu without much preparation prior to the session. On the spot, the team work together to identify what would be increasing or emerging, and what would be decreasing or dying by category on flip charts.

Increasing / Emerging through 20XX	Decreasing / Dying through 20XX
Macro: - Political - Economical - Social - Technological	
Market: Competitors: Partners:	
Customers:	

Some teams don't even bother doing this activity, especially those who already do environmental and market analysis as part of their business planning cycle. So, it's up to the team how to involve future trend search as part of team development effort. The key is to make sure all the members are on the same page and are ready to create the future road map to achieving the team's long-term goal, which will require a bit of a futuristic, helicopter view.

2) **Create a road map:**

This is an exciting exercise for the team to identify the road map or key milestones between now and achieving the mid- to long-term goals. The team will primarily focus on key achievements on the way to the mid-term or long-term goals, 3 to 5 years from now. Some milestones are related to the business outcomes, such as revenue, market share, customer satisfaction, or a new market. Others are concerned with new products and services or innovation items. Some others include the team performance, such as increased team score, team or members, awarded by the industry.

At the beginning of this exercise, the leader needs to make sure all members are on the same page. So, the team will first review the team vision and long-term goals. Then, they will review possible future trends and events to see what will be out there on the way to achieving the goals, which help the team to see what opportunities they can leverage and what risks to avoid or mitigate. Now the team is ready to work on the road map with expanded perspectives and a futuristic mindset.

For co-creating the road map, many teams apply brainstorming using PostIt notes first; individually spending 10 - 15 minutes, and then, they share and expand their ideas, group and integrate ideas, and finalize key achievements they want to see on the way to the goal. Please note that when selecting and prioritizing their ideas, the leader needs to help members focus on big-ticket items, so that it will not become just a shopping list.

Once all the key achievements are identified and agreed on, the team will indicate the key measurement and target timing for achievement. Finally, those selected items for the road map will be placed in the center space of the "Road Map" sheet.

3) **Determine short-term goals**

Once the road map is ready, the team is ready to determine the goals for this year. The leader may guide the discussion to set goals for business outcomes, customer scores, productivity, and team score. Key items could be consistent with the items listed in the long-term goals.

4) **Review current strengths and improvement areas**

After setting the goals for the coming year or the next 6 months, the team will review both customer feedback and team survey results taken during the "Assessment" step.

First, the leader will give a brief overview of survey results, and ask the members to review, discuss, and identify the strengths and improvement areas for the team's services and products for the stakeholders, and record the results on the flip-chart. The team will discuss and agree on the key areas to strengthen or improve.

Second, the team will review the team effectiveness survey results that are shared by the team leader. As with the customer survey results, the team will discuss and identify the strengths and improvement areas for the team and record the them on the flip-chart. The team will discuss and agree on the key areas to strengthen or improve.

As resource and manpower are often limited, the leader needs to be mindful about how much the team can take on and help them select and prioritize their focus items.

5) Determine team actions

The final step or action of "empowering - planning" is determining the team plans for the coming year to meet the expectations of customers and stakeholders (indicated in the customer survey) and also to enhance the team health and performance (indicated in the team survey).

The method of determining the team's actions should be consistent with the one used for determining the road map, using a brainstorming method. Most teams work on a business building action plan focusing on improving customer satisfaction and meeting or exceeding customer needs. Some may identify new services or products. Others will think of innovative processes or systems to provide a better customer experience. After completing the improved business plans, you can shift the energy to work on plans to enhance your team performance, engagement, or productivity, which will, in return, further enhance customer satisfaction.

Once key plans are identified and agreed, the team will discuss and decide the responsible members for each action. The leader needs to ensure that final action plans are fairly allocated among members.

If time permits, each responsible member, develops goals and rough plans to tackle on their selected action items. Then, they introduce their rough implementation ideas to the team, and the team will give feedback to the presenters. (If you don't have time or energy, you may choose to do this portion on a separate day or do this online later, sharing the plan on the team site and gaining input and feedback electronically.)

After sharing the team action plans, the leader will communicate the next steps to finalize the plans and start implementing them to achieve the goals for the next year. You may already inform the format to finalize the action plan, if you already have one.

At the end of the "Empower - Planning" session, the leader and the team review their work so far and celebrate their achievements together. Before closing the session, it's good if each member reflects on the day, identifies their findings, takeaways and indicated actions moving forward; and shares those in the team. Reflection and sharing takeaway with others is key to long-lasting learning and behavioral changes.

Step 4 – Enhance Systems and Enable Members: to build a productive and user-friendly work system and environment and equip members with the necessary competency to operate the new work process and system.

After finalizing the team action plans for the next year, the natural next step is to enhance the team process and environment, as new products and services will usually require improved or modified work processes, systems, or policies. In a way, this can also be preparation for implementing new, strengthened team action plans.

Unless there is a mandate to change the team structure, the initial step for systemic enhancement is process improvement, not structure change or implementing new IT system. Why? For example, if we change and fix the structure or system or roles first, then it will make it hard to change and improve the process, as the structure, roles, or IT system create boundary and rules and override the process.

Also, if the issue is efficiency, not quality, then key steps are to simplify, standardize, and then, mechanize; not the other way around. There is no point in mechanizing or systemizing a complicated process that has overwrap activities.

Basic Flows:

1) **Improve or build better processes** – The key to the successful identification of effective processes is to focus on meeting or exceeding customer expectation of the output or services of the team. Poor processes are usually built around sub-optimization, which is based on the needs of the provider. To avoid sub-optimization, we need to involve all key stakeholders in the process mapping, so that all are aligned on the final output and the customer or stakeholder requirements.

   Once the team and key stakeholders get together, are aligned on the final output, and know the customer requirements and needs, they brainstorm necessary activities to deliver the expected output. Next, they put those activities into the most productive and efficient sequence. Then, the team will decide measurements for each activity to ensure successful operation without sub-optimization.

2) **Determine structure and roles** - Once the team is aligned to the key activities, sequence, and measures, they will discuss and determine how those activities should be structured and who should do them, regardless of the current structure and roles. A responsible person or group needs to be chosen based on their capability.

3) **Determine the systems, policy, and guidelines** - Now the team needs to determine any new systems and policy to be implemented to support effective operation of the new process. This will complete the planning phase of the new or improved process for the team's new product or services.

4) **Communication through various media** - Now, the team needs to identify the most effective communication plans to ensure all stakeholders understand the new plan. Effective communication is vital for successful implementation of the new process.

5) **Enable the team** - As the work process, system, measurement, policy, and guidelines are changed, we need to help the team master and get ready for implementing the new or improved work processes. This will include lots of practice and rehearsal to make sure the team can implement the new plan perfectly.

6) **Prepare the necessary system and environment** - This is about preparing and implementing or installing new systems or hard elements to support the new product or service launch.

7) **Implement new processes** - Upon completion of sufficient practice and successful test-runs, we will implement the plan.

Step 5 – Track the progress and consolidate the plans and system: to ensure the successful execution of the team action plans to help achieve the team mission, vision, and values.

There are three key activities in this step.

1) What gets measured gets done. So, the team will keep tracking and reviewing their progress on a periodical basis. If we don't track and review the progress, we can easily slip and miss the mark, and we may not be able to achieve the intended goals of the team. Progress review is a great opportunity for identifying further improvement or strengthening opportunities.

2) Once the team identifies issues, improvement areas, or even team development opportunities, such as strengthening relationships and team cohesion, along with the member or leader changes. Then, the team should tackle the issues and consolidate the plan and systems to maximize the team performance.

3) Along with the progress review and plan improvement, the team is to share and record its learnings and celebrate the progress.

In Summary

We reviewed the four phases of team development introduced by Tuckman – forming, storming, norming, and performing. Leaders need to ascertain which phase their team is in, as that will help prepare them for their team development focus area.

Basic team development steps are: (1) assess, (2) engage and envision, (3) empower, (4) enhance systems and enable team members, and (5) track the progress and consolidate the plans and systems.

Assess: the assessment of the situation is the very key to the success of the team's development, as we can identify what to do by understanding what our strengths and weaknesses are. For the assessment to be effective, it needs to be holistic and systemic, by involving all the members and stakeholders and in gaining their perspectives and feedback on the current team performance.

Engage and Envision: The leader needs to be sure all the members are engaged. If not, they need to do some engaging work, involving several mutual understanding activities. Once the team has built basic engagement, the leader can move to alignment work to get the team involved in co-creating an inspiring team mission, vision, values, and strategic focus area(s).

Empower: In this step, the leader guides the team to co-develop key plans, goals, and roles, often done through a 1-day workshop. When the team is aligned with the game plans, then, off they go to implement the plans.

Enhance systems and enable the team: The next steps are to build productive work systems and an environment to deliver the above plans. While we already seem to have all the systems and environments, we have always some improvement areas in our work processes and systems in the team. Then, we need to equip the team with the needed competency to run the new systems.

The final step is to track the progress and consolidate the plans and system. High performing teams have a robust tracking mechanism to consistently deliver expected results. This will also help the team build high performing and learning cultures as well as building members and the team capability.

Again, there is no one best approach that works in every situation, as there are so many variables in business, teams and external environments. To build a high-performance team. we need to engage members, envision the ideal future, empower our members and enhance our work systems and environment, which ever factors are the driving forces. The leader needs to trust and unleash members potential, and borrow their thoughts and ideas to strengthen the team.

Chapter 10

Upgrading Your Skills as a Leader

I hope you have enjoyed reading this book to learn how to make your team happier and more productive. Up until Chapter 9, we have reviewed the current issues and challenges in today's work environment – engagement, productivity and culture, team effectiveness factors, leadership foundations, leaders' 5 actions to create happy and productive teams, and how to put those actions to enhance your team. As the leader is a key driver for a team's success, I will discuss how to upgrade your leadership mindset and competency in this last Chapter.

When I was in Marketing, I think I was a good manager, building brand and business, but I wasn't a great, or high impact manager. As mentioned in the Introduction, although I thought I was a very good people manager, I was not. I put a good amount of energy to develop my direct reports and team primarily through giving a stretch assignment, teaching and coaching. But I wasn't so flexible in responding to various kinds of development needs of members and the team.

I've grown a lot from taking lots of new actions to help lots of teams build better cultures. I certainly had a lot of insights from coaching and feedbacks from various boss in my prior career. I also learned a wide variety of practical theories, principles and tools from various leadership and organization experts around the world after becoming an external leadership and organization development facilitator. So, I want to share some of my learnings through my leadership journey in this Chapter. And I am hopeful that this final Chapter will assist you to gain additional ideas to further strengthen your leadership capacity.

Leadership Vision

Our image is our reality. We become what we think of ourselves; good or bad. If we think we are small, we become a small leader. On the other hand, if we think we are resourceful and great, we become a great leader. Our image and our intention create our reality. So, what kind of leader do you want to be? What achievements do you intend to make as a great leader? Setting the right intention and goals will be effective first steps to growing and attaining your desired results. Poor leaders do not have a clear leadership vision. So, make your inspiring leadership vision as clear and vivid as possible. If you are not inspired by your vision, you will not be motivated to get there. If your vision is unclear and vague, you can't find your path to get there.

INTENTION ➡ ATTENTION ➡ BEHAVIORS ➡ RESULTS

So, what do you intend to achieve and leave as your legacy in your team or organization? Business? People? Team and organization? How do you make sure whether or not you have achieved your goals or made a success? Your SMART goals as a leader? What experiences do you need to get there? Who are with you when you achieved those results? What are they saying about your achievements? What resources did you use? How do you feel when accomplishing those outcomes? What competency do you need to have to achieve those great successes? What kind of mindset do you have to lead your team and business as a leader?

Leadership Competency

A Leader's effectiveness is a good barometer of their team's effectiveness. The more effective the leader is, the higher performing the team is. Now, I want to touch on leadership competency, leadership derailers, and how to strengthen competency, so you will be able to implement your plans and achieve your ideal team vision effectively.

So, what skills do we need as a leader to build business, grow our members, and develop the team, taking both managerial and leadership actions? What is the skill set required for leaders in your organization? Or what kind of leadership competency model does your organization use?

There are many leadership competency models. In fact, many large companies have their own leadership model, or a set of competencies expected for the leader, and use them to evaluate and develop their leaders. While using different vocabularies for leader's competencies, more than half of the skill sets of those different leadership competency models are similar.

One of the oldest leadership models is the one introduced by Robert Katz, it was introduced in Harvard Business Review in 1955. While it's more than 60 years old, his model is still valid in today's business world. He indicated there are three dimensions of the competency leaders need to perform, i.e., technical, human skills, and conceptual skills.

The technical skill includes those needed to effectively perform functional tasks to deliver their business results, such as selling skills for sales managers, programming skills for system engineering leaders, instructional design skills for training managers, which also includes technical and industry knowledge. The human skill is about working with and leading others effectively, such as communication, relationship-building, influencing, and conflict management skills. The conceptual skill is pertaining to thinking and developing ideas and plans, ranging from creating a vision, developing a strategy, seeing a holistic view of the business, making judgments, and solving problems.

While all the three skill dimensions are important, upper management needs stronger conceptual skills than middle managers and supervisors, whereas the supervisors and middle managers need stronger technical skills compared to upper management; and human skills are consistently important regardless of the levels of the leaders. Although Kat's model is simply grouped into three dimensions, most leadership skills can be categorized into those three dimensions.

For more recent leadership competency models, I want to introduce you to the Zenger-Folkman model, as their model is developed from on their field research, not based on some guru's personal experiences. Zenger and Folkman have globally researched more than 25,000 senior managers and executives and asked their members about their manager's strengths and behavioral characteristics, using multi-rater feedback, not via a simple self-rating by managers. Their research (2002) indicates there are five categories of leadership competency, and those who perform extremely effectively in multiple areas, outperform as a leader and deliver exceptional results. Within five categories, there are 16 leadership competencies (please see a separate list on the following page). Five leadership competency categories are as below.

1. **Character** - exhibiting integrity - constantly doing the right things to role model the right mindset and behaviors. This will help create the right culture in the organization.
2. **Personal capability** - exhibiting problem-solving skills, innovation, and self-development skills in addition to technical expertise.
3. **Delivering results** - strong results-orientation which helps deliver expected results or overachieve targets despite challenges and obstacles.
4. **Interpersonal skills** - ability to effectively communicate with others, build trusting relationships, motivate and develop others, and build teamwork.
5. **Change leadership** - skills to envision and successfully lead change.

Importantly, great leaders are great learners. As customer needs, competitive landscape, and technologies are changing rapidly, teams and organizations need to be agile in terms of learning and taking new actions. We cannot survive and thrive in this fast-paced, global economy if leaders are not improving, innovating, and transcending themselves constantly. Continuously learning leaders are must-haves to build a learning culture in the team. If the leaders stop learning, that will send the wrong message to members that learning is not important in their teams. So, what new things have you learned in the last 3 months? And, how did you use that newly learned competency in the workplace to increase your team's performance?

Building on positive psychology, the primary leadership development focus is to maximize one's strengths, not on fixing the problems. So, leaders need to identify their strengths, so they can further strengthen their strong skill set to enhance their leadership results and performance.

Which competency category and skill set are your strengths? Which ones are your improvement opportunities? And, to be an exemplary leader, which skill area(s) would you like to further strengthen to lead your team to be a success? Please rate your skills on a 5-point scale, using the check list on the next page. (5: Exceptionally great, 4: Good, 3: Almost good, 2: Not so good, 1: Poor)

The 16 Skills of Highly Effective Leaders	Rating
1. Character	
1. Displaying high integrity and honesty	
2. Personal capability	
2. Technical & professional skills	
3. Solving problems and analyzing issues	
4. Innovation	
5. Practicing self-development	
3. Focusing on results	
6. Focus on results (and do everything possible to meet goals)	
7. Establish stretch goals	
8. Go beyond what needs to be done	
4. Interpersonal skills	
9. Communicating powerfully and prolifically	
10. Inspiring and motivating others to high performance	
11. Building relationships	
12. Developing others	
13. Collaboration and teamwork	
5. Leading change	
14. Developing strategic perspectives	
15. Championing change	
16. Connecting internal groups with external experts	

Nevertheless, if the weakness is at a fatal level, leaders need to make an improvement in those areas. Zenger and Folkman's research also identified five types of fatal flaws which made a leader step down. 5 fatal flaws are as follows:

1) **Inability to learn from mistakes** - They do not understand whether or not they made a mistake, and thus, they cannot learn anything from their mistakes. They likely make the same mistakes continuously.

2) **Interpersonal incompetence** - They cannot build relationships with others, and they cannot communicate and positively influence others.

3) **Lack of openness to new ideas** - They are not open to others' ideas if that is new or different from their own. They insist on their own ideas or ways of doing things.

4) **Tendency to blame others for problems** - They lack in accountability, and when things don't go well, they tend to blame others.

5) **Lack of initiative** - They like to continue doing what's worked in the past, and they are not proactively taking new initiatives.

As the above fatal flaws suggest, the research indicates interpersonal skills are key development areas for many leaders - many failing leaders have a tendency of lack of interpersonal skills, such as building trust or active listening skills. As we already reviewed, without solid interpersonal skills, leaders cannot build healthy and collaborative relationships in the team, so the team will not perform well and may collapse eventually.

If in case you have development opportunities in interpersonal skills, four skills you may want to build are: (1) active listening, (2) questioning, (3) messaging, and (4) mindfulness. Those are four skills I have especially practiced after I left the corporate life. Skill development is just like learning a new sport, and it is best done through learning, practicing, modeling and actually using on the job. The more we practice and use new skills on the job or life, we build less used muscles and the flexibility to perform better.

First, I often hear from employees from various industries complaining about poor listening managers. Active listening is about truly focusing on the other party and actively and empathetically listening to what they are saying, feeling, and experiencing. Active listeners can fully understand others, so they can take correct actions immediately. This is one of keys for many leaders to enhance interpersonal skills.

Active listening is not our natural skill, so we need to practice daily. Keys to active listening are:

1) Focus on others 100%
2) Eye contact
3) Respect and empathize
4) Be interested in others
5) Eliminate self-talk

Second, powerful questioning is also very important for leaders to understand member's ideas, concerns, or dreams. Poor managers primarily use closed-ended questions and leading questions and learn little from members. Good managers use lots of open-ended questions to understand member's situations and thoughts. Great managers also use exploring and thought-provoking questions to help others expand their perspectives and identify better solutions for themselves. One way you can improve your questioning skills is to turn statements you want to make into questions, and ask questions to members, instead of telling your thoughts. Questioning is usually more effective in influencing others than telling, as it helps members think through, understand, and make decisions.

So, ask powerful open-ended questions when:

- You want to tell something to your team
- You want to help others grow
- You want to recommend something to others
- You want to redirect others' focus
- You want to change others' thinking
- You want others to do something for you
- You don't like what you saw or heard
- You want others to explore alternatives

Third, there are several forms of messaging – directing, persuading, empowering, and inspiring. All forms have a situation to use them effectively. "Directing" is best used when there is an urgent action to take, such as when stakeholders are in a deep problem and need immediate help, and there's no time to discuss with the team. "Persuasion" is suited for when the situation requires a logical explanation and evidence to get buy-in from stakeholders and members. "Empowering" is suited for the situation where participants are basically capable and want to participate in planning and implementing some actions. "Inspiring" is good when some demand for change exists in the situation, and stakeholders hope to see a clear vision for the change. Which one of the four forms is your default style? As most of us have a default mode, a good way to strengthen your messaging power is to identify and work on less used styles, so you can address broader situations. For your information, there are more managers who use directing and persuading when talking with members.

Different Messaging Styles

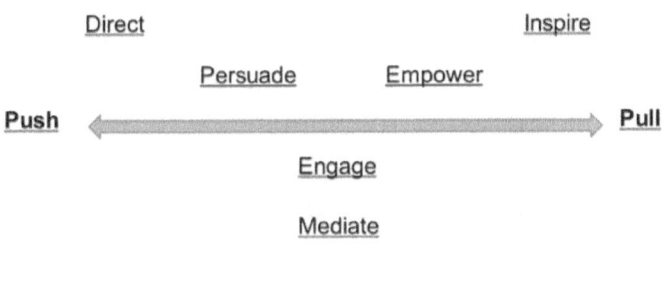

Lastly, a mindfulness skill is highly expected for leaders of poor engagement and stressful teams. What is mindfulness, anyway? Mindfulness is paying attention to and being aware of what's happening right now, both inside and outside ourselves, in a holistic, non-judgmental and balanced manner. The key benefits of being mindful are; (1) improved decision-making as we have broader and more rational information, more balanced perspectives, and more focused mindset; (2) more stable, calm, and less emotional, even in a devastating situation; (3) less anxiety and frustration from day-to-day challenges and frustrations. There are lots of ways to practice mindfulness, and meditation is one of simple and effective ways to learn to be more mindful. Research by Harvard neuroscientists indicates doing seated meditation for 20 minutes a day for 8 weeks can enhance our thinking, concentration, and resiliency (Hölzel, Carmody, Vangel, Congleton, Yerramsetti, Gard and Lazar, 2011). I certainly recommend you try some mindful practices more than once a week for 2 months. You will be able to see its effectiveness yourself.

So, what is your priority for strengthening and improvement skills? What will you be doing right now? Once you identify your focal strengthening skill, please start new habit and behavior right away. Recent research by the NeuroLeadership Institute indicates we need one to six months to make a new behavior a habit, depending on its complexity. Good practice makes perfect. And, effective leaders are agile, so they take a new action immediately to make a positive change sooner rather than later. Please identify and indicate your strengthening/improvement areas and new actions, and your expected results (specific, measurable, achievable, and relevant goals and time bound) in below chart.

Strengthening Areas & New Actions	SMART Goals (How Measure?)
1:	
2:	
3:	

Dr. Marshall Goldsmith suggests that we should build and practice new leadership habits everyday to getting better at them; and if we continue practicing and reflecting those habits everyday, we will certainly become a better boss in 6 weeks or so. Journaling your intent and results everyday can also help us grow. It can be just one line, not even a paragraph. Spending just a few minutes on this is not a bad idea to keep us moving forward in our leadership development journey.

In Summary

In today's fast-changing global economy, all leaders need to constantly advance their capability and capacity. Great leaders are great learners. They have a clear picture of their ideal leader, and they are passionate about continuously growing to becoming their ideal. That's why they keep growing, to keep up with ever-changing stakeholders' needs and wants, and deliver business, people, and team results through the five key leaders' actions – engaging, envisioning, empowering, enabling, and enhancing. They possess multiple skillsets, ranging from problem-solving skills to interpersonal skills, to change leadership skills to result-orientation.

Also, leadership character of integrity is crucially important to building credibility. Interpersonal skills are also important to building engaging and psychologically safe teams, which are often associated with a fatal flaw of failing leaders.

Building on a positive psychology, we should first focus on identifying and strengthening our strongest skills, rather than fixing weaknesses. However, if you find some fatal flaw based on team member and customer feedback, you should work to eliminate those derailers, as that will certainly help build your credibility as well as your leadership competency.

I am sure you have fundamental and important knowledge and know how about building a happy and productive team. I am also hopeful that you know how to grow and upgrade your skills as a leader. And I believe you will start new leadership habits today to make your team happier and more productive. I look forward to hearing from you about your new actions, habits, and better results in your team soon!

Bon voyage!

Bibliography

Agarwal, P. and Farndale, Elaine, High performance work systems and creativity implementation: the role of psychological capital and psychological safety, *Human Resource Management Journal*, 27, 3, (440-458), (2017).

Ariani, D. W., (2015). Relationship with Supervisor and Co-Workers, Psychological Condition and Employee Engagement in the Workplace; Journal of Business and Management Volume 4, Issue 3 (2015), 34-47

Barge, J. K. (1996). Leadership skills and the dialectics of leadership in group decision making. In R. Y. Hirokawa & M. S. Poole (Eds.), *Communication and group decision making*

(2nd ed., pp. 301-342). Thousand Oaks, CA: Sage.

Bartlett, K. R., & Kang, D. S. (2004). Training in organizational commitment in response to industry and organizational change in New Zealand and the United States. *Human Resource Development International, 7*(4), 423-440

Goldsmith, M, & Reiter, M., (2007). *What Got You Here Won't Get You There: How Successful People Become Even More Successful.* New York: Hachette Book

Goleman, D. (2000). Leadership that gets results. *Boston, MA: Harvard Business Review. March-April (pp. 82-83).*

Green, C. H., & Howe, A. P. (2012). *The trusted advisor fieldbook: a comprehensive toolkit for leading with trust.* Hoboken, NJ: John Wiley & Sons, Inc.

Hackman, J. R. (1990). Work teams in organizations: An orienting framework. In J. R. Hackman (Ed.), *Groups that work (and those that don't): Creating conditions for effective teamwork* (pp. 1-14). San Francisco, CA: Jossey-Bass.

Hackman, J. R., & Walton, R. E. (1986). Leading groups in organizations. In P. S. Goodman & Associates (Eds.), *Designing effective work groups* (pp. 72-119). San Francisco, CA: Jossey-Bass.

Hanna, D. P. (1988). Designing organizations for high performance. Addison-Wesley Publishing Company

Hölzel, B. K., Carmody, J., Vangel, M., Congleton, C., Yerramsetti, S. M., Gard, T., & Lazar, S. W. (2011). Mindfulness practice leads to increases in regional brain gray matter density. Psychiatry Research: Neuroimaging, 191(1), 36-43

Katz, R. L.(1955). Skills of an effective administrator. *Harvard Business Review 33*(1), 33-42

Kaye, B. & Jordan-Evans, S. (2005). *Love'em, or lose'em.* San Francisco, CA: Berrett-Koehler Publishers, Inc.

Kotter, J. P. (1990). *A force for change: How leadership differs from management.* New York: Free Press.

Kozlowski, S. W. J., & Ilgen, D. R. (2006). Enhancing the effectiveness of work groups and teams. *Psychological Science in the Public Interest, 7*(3), 77-124.

LaFasto, F. M. J., & Larson, C. E. (2001). *When team work best: 6,000 team members and leaders tell what it takes to succeed.* Thousand Oaks, CA: Sage.

Larson, C. E., & LaFasto, F. M. J. (1989). *Teamwork: What must go right/what can go wrong.* Newbury Park, CA: Sage.

Lencioni, P. (2011). *Overcoming the five dysfunctions of a team: a field guide for leaders, managers, and facilitators.* San Francisco. CA: Jossey-Bass.

McCauley, C. D., Moxley, R. S., & Velsor, E V. (1998). *The center for creative leadership: Handbook of leadership development.* San Francisco. CA: Jossey-Bass.

McGrath, J. E., Arrow, H., & Berdahl, J. L. (2000). The study of groups: past, present, and future. *Personality and Social Psychology Review, 4*(1), 95-105.

Mathieu, J. E., Heffner, T. S., Goodwin, G. F., Salas, E., & Cannon-Bowers, J. A. (2000). The influence of shared mental models on team process and performance. *Journal of Applied Psychology, 85*(2), 273-283.

Northouse, P. (2005) Leadership: theory and practices

Schein, E. H. (2004). *Organizational culture and leadership.* San Francisco. CA: Jossey-Bass.

Trist, E.L., G.W. Higgin, H. Murray and A.B. Pollock. (1963). Organizational 1963/Vol. II Trist, Higgin, Murray and Pollock

Trist, E. L. (1981). *The evolution of socio-technical systems: a conceptual framework and an action research program.* Occasional paper no. 2. Ontario Quality of Working Life Center

Tuckman, B. W., & Jenson, M. A. (1977). Stages of small group development revisited. *Group and Organization Studies, 2,* 419-427.

Webber, S. S. (2002). Leadership and trust facilitating cross-functional team success. *Journal of Management Development, 21*(3), 201-214.

Weldon, E., Jehn, K. A., & Pradhan, P. (1991). Process that mediates the relationship between a group goal and improved group performance. *Journal of Personality & Social Psychology, 61*(4), 555-569.

Zaccaro, S. J., Rittman, A. L., & Marks, M. A. (2001). Team Leadership. <u>*The Team Leadership Quarterly*</u>, *12*, 451-483.

Zenger, J. H., & Folkman, J. (2002). *The extraordinary leader: turning good managers into great leaders.* New York: McGraw-Hill

Author Bio

Yoshiharu (Yoshi) Matsui is the founder of HPO Creation, a consulting firm specializing in leadership and organization development. He is passionate about building happy and productive organizations on the planet by supporting leaders and executives to become more effective in creating more engaged, productive, and connected teams and organizations, where members perform lively, confidently, and collaboratively to their full potential.

Since 2003, Yoshi has facilitated and coached thousands of leaders and leadership teams to strengthen their performance, resulting in a significantly improved employee engagement and performance. Past clients have included AstraZeneca, Bayer, Diageo, Goldman Sachs, Hilton International, LVMH, Magna, Manulife, Pfizer, Schott, Springer, Swarovski, Victrex, and many more. He also teaches leadership development and organization change at Temple University.

Prior to becoming an external facilitator and consultant, Yoshi had more than 10 years of marketing management experience with record sales for several products along with 10 years of Human Resources and Organization Development management experience at various global companies, such as Procter & Gamble, Levi Strauss, and Nortel Networks. He is a certified master coach, organization assessor, and a certified Human Resource Management Professional. He is also certified in several assessment tools, such as TriMetrix, DiSC, MBTI, and Facet5. He holds an MBA from Northwest Missouri State University and a Doctoral degree in Education in Organization Change from Pepperdine University, USA.

www.ingramcontent.com/pod-product-compliance
Lightning Source LLC
Chambersburg PA
CBHW031606210526
45464CB00004B/1452